RUSSIANS OBSERVED

RUSSIANS OBSERVED

by

JOHN LAWRENCE

HODDER AND STOUGHTON

Printed in Great Britain for Hodder and Stoughton Limited,
St. Paul's House, Warwick Lane, London, E.C.4
by Ebenezer Baylis and Son, Ltd.,
The Trinity Press, Worcester, and London

Preface

This is a personal book. If I were writing an Anatomy of Russia or Anatomy of the Soviet Union, the balance of the book would be different. I should describe the lives of workers and peasants, of high officials and dwellers in forced labour camps. The precise address of about a hundred of these institutions is known, and there must be others. I should give religion its place, but not quite the place it has here. And in describing Russia's religious life, I should examine the evidence about the underground and illegal Churches and about opposition tendencies in the legal Churches. I should not unsay anything in this book, but I should add to it. I could, indeed, describe many aspects of Soviet life from good second-hand evidence, but this is a book of first-hand experience. I have seen what I have seen; and that is what I describe in these pages.

My comparisons are inevitably drawn from those places that I know best, and I was born and brought up in southern and south-west England, though my ancestry is Irish. I apologise to readers who do not know the same places, but Chelsea and the King's Road are now known to very wide circles in other lands through T.V. and fashion magazines.

I am grateful to all who have read my typescript in whole or part and especially to my wife, my brother, my publishers, G. S. Fraser, Paddy Fraser, Peter Reddaway and John Wilkins. I am equally grateful to Margaret Ford, who has typed the whole book. All of them have given useful advice about content or presentation.

J.W.L.

Contents

Contents

CHAPTER I

Introduction

This book is about Russians seen from eye level. It is skimmed from the observations of half a lifetime and most of it is taken from letters and diaries made while scenes were fresh in my mind. I have felt obliged for the sake of politeness, if no more, to change some names and places but I have been as careful as I can to give all significant detail exactly as it occurred. This is not a book of Kremlinology. Indeed Kremlinology only interests me to a moderate extent. Nor can I describe the Soviet under-world from first-hand experience. This is a book of direct observations and I have no direct knowledge of what goes on either behind the screen of security which hides high Soviet functionaries from common eyes, or behind the barbed wire and wooden watch-towers of concentration camps. This gives the book its value, if any, and its limitations. In my book *A History of Russia* (Mentor Books, new edition 1969) I have tried to give the essence of events, drawing on what I have read and heard from others as well as on what I have seen, but here I concentrate on the concrete reality that I have seen with my eyes and heard with my ears. I have taken such chances as came my way, but every man's experience is incomplete; so, here I do not even attempt to give a completely balanced picture, as I do in my *History*.

In particular in this book I give more space than might be expected to describing Russian religious life. There are two reasons for this. First, religion is a more important part of the texture of Soviet life than is commonly realised, and it is becoming more important. And secondly, I have some special knowledge and experience of the subject. Religion has been neglected by many previous writers for several reasons. Until very recently the people one met most easily were out of earshot of the Church, or if they had religious interests they were likely to have good reasons for keeping this from foreigners. I do not wish to exaggerate the influence of religion in the Soviet Union but the facts which I give about the influence of the Orthodox Church and of the Baptists ought to be taken into account in any description of the Soviet Union that purports to be realistic. So it seemed right to paint this part of the picture in some detail.

It will be seen that I do not accept uncritically the view that apostate official Churches manipulated by an atheist government stand over against a true Christianity maintained by underground groups. Such a view oversimplifies a complex situation. There are undoubted ambiguities in the rôle of certain Church functionaries and Church organisations, but this does not prevent devoted Christians from working within the officially recognised churches. Moreover, one should bear in mind the probability, amounting almost to certainty, that the secret police have penetrated the underground Church organisations, as well as the official Churches, both Orthodox and Baptist. One of the standing problems of Soviet life is to find an honest path through ambiguous situations; and the Church shares this problem with writers, scientists, industrial managers, workers, and peasants, in a word, with all Soviet citizens. Having said this, it is only fair to add that the leaders of the group who have broken away from the official Baptist Church remain in prison or in exile, which is *prima facie* evidence of their incorruptibility. A full exposition of these matters would take me outside the limits of this book, but my views are on record in *A History of Russia* and in what I have written over many years in the quarterly magazine *Frontier*, which I edit.

Writing this book has been like painting a still life. I gaze with concentration on what is before my eyes, until the salient features stand out. Then I try to put them down faithfully. I select, but I try not to distort. Chardin is the model for this kind of writing, not Braque. My aim is more modest than Braque's. In the last chapter I deliberately stand back from my material and try to assess the drift of history as it is unfolding. I do not aspire to prophecy, but one must try to discern the chief forces at work in one's own age, so that one may be ready for the future. I know that on previous occasions my analysis of these forces has interested people in various parts of eastern Europe. I believe, however, that chance plays a great part in history. The future is genuinely open. Accurate prediction would be impossible, even if one knew all the facts.

I have deliberately made this a book about Russians, not about the other peoples of the Soviet Union. The Russians are the most important element in the Soviet Union, and it is the Russians that I know.

I am often asked why it is that I have been allowed to travel so freely and to see so much in the Soviet Union over so long a period, while many writers and journalists have had obstacles put in their way. I have, indeed, had much kindness from the Soviet authorities. I have never had a visa refused and often, though not always, I have been allowed to go where I wanted. What is the reason? I can only guess, but my guess may at least give some sardonic amusement to the K.G.B., as the former Cheka, then O.G.P.U., then N.K.V.D., then M.V.D., etc., etc., is now called. I was very carefully checked for security by the Soviet authorities during the war, when I was working at the British Embassy in a capacity that gave unusual opportunities for contact with Russians, and I know that I was given a good report. I never concealed my views, though I tried not to obtrude them unsuitably; this, evidently, was not resented. The Soviet secret police is an odious organisation but not all its servants are vile. I knew that everything I said or did was liable to be reported. So, I said nothing I did not want reported, and on occasions I used this line of communication to say things that I wanted to be passed on. I could see that at first the most complicated and devious motives were attributed to me. I countered by behaving in a completely straightforward manner. I am sure that this is the most effective way to deal with Soviet officialdom, as well as being better for other reasons. I reasoned that if some of the people I was dealing with were devious and I was not, that would give me an advantage. And if I saw through any little games, I always showed it, though more often by the lift of an eyebrow or the inflection of my voice than by any words I used. On the other hand I always gave credit where credit was due, even if it went against the case I was making. After the war I thought that the Soviet Union must be firmly contained by N.A.T.O., but I also thought that the western powers had foolishly given Stalin some reasons for his suspicions, groundless though I believed these to be. I thought his fears of the west were real; I said so; and some Communist spokesmen used to quote me. Finally, when I was living in the Soviet Union I never listened to anti-Soviet talk; for one thing it was likely to be provocation; so I choked it off at once. The Soviet authorities may not like all that I say, but they know that I will not twist anything against them. But of course I am not the only student of Russia to behave circumspectly. I have been lucky.

So far, so good. But I know that I am expendable. On every visit to Russia I know that I would be framed, if it suited the K.G.B. to do so. I reckon, however, that it would not suit them, and I hope the calculation is correct. I should be sad if I could not visit the Soviet Union again. Nor, on the other hand, do I want to die in Siberia.

Russia has drawn me since my teens, since the days when one read *Anna Karenina* in French, because French translations of Russian novels were thought to be better than Constance Garnett's. But until I went to work in the Soviet Union in 1942, I had no idea that so much of my life would be bound up with Russia. Now it is in my blood and I could not get rid of it, even if I would.

Everyone who knows Russia has ambiguous feelings. Once after a particularly awful Soviet day a friend said to me, "You don't really like Russia, do you?" I had to say, "No-one likes Russia. Either you hate it or you love it, and more probably both." In my case love predominates. No-one whose eyes are open could like that grey exterior, but look below the surface and you find something different. It takes practice to see clearly in that conflicting light, and the only thing I claim as an observer is that I have been training my eyes for half a lifetime to see Russian realities. The process has made me increasingly wary and sometimes cynical. On a long view my hopes are undimmed, but with every year that passes I am more appalled by the suffering, the cruelty, and the corruption of the past fifty years. On re-reading what I have written about Russia over more than twenty years I am struck by the *naïveté* of some of my earlier deductions, as well as by some observations which I still find interesting.

My first visit to Russia was no more than a ranging shot. I went as a tourist in April 1934. I was very green but even so it gives an added perspective to have seen the Soviet Union before the Great Terror that followed Kirov's murder a few months after my visit. In these days Marxist idealism was alive; and it was an open question whether capitalism was not sinking beneath its structural contradictions during the great depression of the 'thirties. So I looked at Russia with keen interest. I had been told it would be drab, and drab it was. Such simple things attracted a crowd. At one of the crossings of the Nevsky Prospekt in Leningrad a sizeable crowd had collected to watch the policeman control the sparse traffic. He was a man with strongly Mongolian features and he waved his truncheon with the panache of a drum major with his baton. That was all, but I was told that people came every day to see him perform. Shortages could produce surprising innovations. More than once I saw people wearing overcoats of cow hide which showed the pattern of the cow's coat.

In those days foreigners were expected to pay for many things in foreign exchange. So I equipped myself with some dollars and on the train between Riga and Moscow I went along to the restaurant car and ordered a cup of tea. I took out a dollar and waited for the change, while the attendant went away and wrote for quite a long time. When he came back he gave me two Belgian francs, a few Polish zloty, a few Hungarian pengos, three Finnish marks and half-a-crown. This was my first introduction to the complication of getting the simplest things done in the Soviet Union. Later I went to get a snack and the attendant went away and wrote even longer. I waited with patient curiosity and eventually he proposed a deal: "You give me another dollar, I'll give you two German marks, you give me a shilling, I'll give you x zloty and y heller, you have another glass of tea and we'll call it quits."

I had booked my tour outside the Soviet Union through a travel agency, who were the accredited representatives of Intourist, after looking the trains up myself in a Soviet time-table. It seemed to fit in nicely. After a stay in Moscow we would take the night train to Leningrad, change at Chudovo at seven a.m. and take what seemed quite a convenient train to Novgorod where we were booked for two or three nights; after that we were going on to Leningrad. I had paid for all this in advance and checked it with Intourist's representative. But it was not as simple as that. When we got to Moscow they said almost at once, "When are you going to Leningrad?" I answered, "We are going to Novgorod first." "But you go to Leningrad first." "I know most people do, but we are going to Novgorod first." "But you go to Leningrad first." "Yes, but we are going to Novgorod." "Then you had better see the manager."

I saw the manager and had exactly the same conversation with him. By this time my curiosity was roused and I decided to try and find out what was going on. In the end I had an interview with the deputy head of the whole of Intourist, a charming English-speaking Jew who was liquidated in the Terror not long afterwards. "What can I do for you?" "You see we have got these tickets to Novgorod and . . ." "But you go to Leningrad." "I know most people do, but we have specially booked our tour this way round." "It can't be done." "Why not?" "It can't be done." "But here are our tickets. I shall get on the train at Moscow and get out at Chudovo at seven a.m. That is the time when the train stops at Chudovo isn't it?" "Yes, but you would have to wait there." "All right." "You might have to wait a long time." "How long?" "Three or four weeks." "You mean that the train in the time-table doesn't exist?" "No it doesn't. I am always telling them to take it out of the time-table but they think it looks bad to have a line without any regular trains." That was the first thing that taught me to question appearances, but I did not find that every locked cupboard contained a skeleton. When they showed me a rest house at Leningrad, where people who were overworked could be sent to recuperate, I asked to see the kitchen. This caused consternation verging on panic, but after some hurried whispering I was shown in. Everyone wore spotless white coats, as in a hospital, and they were cooking minced cutlets that looked better than what we got at our own hotel.

We did get to Novgorod. They gave us a car from Leningrad, starting at four o'clock in the morning and we bumped our way through mud and pot-holes over a scarcely existent road. The sky was lovely with a watery sun between pale clouds but the countryside was dreary. The spring floods were up, but in that latitude the trees still had their buds tightly glued up. The collectivisation of agriculture was in the very recent past, the peasants had killed most of their stock, including their horses, but the tractors which were meant to take the place of horses had not arrived and would not arrive in sufficient numbers for several years more. You could tell a collective farm from an uncollectivised village, if any of these had been left, simply by the fact that it had a long, low wooden building to house such livestock as had escaped slaughter by their previous owners before they were taken over by the collective. And that was all the difference that I could see.

We arrived at Novgorod late in the morning and began to sight-see avidly. There was St. Sophia looking just as it does in Eisenstein's film, *Alexander Nevsky*, which was at that time an exciting novelty; and there were the red brick walls of the Kremlin reflected in the flood waters of the river Volkhov.

We were given a good simple lunch at a spotlessly clean hostel, where we would gladly have stayed, and then they tried to drive us home. But the sun was shining and I insisted on taking a boat to row across the flood waters to the twelfth-century church of the Nereditsa, tragically destroyed in the second world war. The boatman sang the song of Stenka Razin and we were accompanied by a local girl who discoursed eloquently about the glories of mediaeval Republican Novgorod. Here one felt in touch with a Russia that was older than the Revolution, older than gunpowder. At this time the "old wooden Rus" of the poet Yesemin, Isadora Duncan's lover, had not quite disappeared.

After this we started back to Moscow late and the car soon broke a spring which rattled against the chassis like a machine gun every time we hit a pot-hole. The road was so bumpy and we jolted so violently that by two a.m. when we got home, after twenty-two hours on the go, our behinds were as sore as if we had been severely beaten.

Both at Novgorod and in Moscow we visited the State Restoration Workshops where they were cleaning and restoring mediaeval icons. Russia led the world in this. The rediscovery of mediaeval icons came a few years before the Revolution and the work of cleaning and restoration has been continued ever since. Previously smoke from the icon lamps had obscured the icons, so that they had to be repainted about once a century. Of course the style of painting changed completely and all memory of the great painting of previous ages had disappeared. I remember being shown one icon of the fourteenth century from which five subsequent paintings had been removed, and each layer had been carefully preserved and transferred to a separate surface, so that you could see all the stages side by side. The man who had carried out this work asked me back to his flat. Even then I knew a little Russian, though not enough for a sustained conversation. Soon after this the Terror made such casual contacts between foreigners and Russians impossible.

CHAPTER II

Russians in War Time

I next saw the Soviet Union at war, and it is this experience that has made the most lasting impression. Old Moscow hands are typed by the period at which they first got to know the Soviet Union. Those who arrived in 1937–8 still measure everything by the Terror; those who knew the Nep in the 'twenties made that their standard. I belong to the war generation and see everything in the Soviet Union in the light of the three years from 1942 to 1945, when I was Press Attaché at the British Embassy, first in the wartime capital at Kuibyshev on the middle Volga, and then in Moscow. I arrived with two colleagues at Murmansk in the far north, having been torpedoed near Spitzbergen. I owned what I wore and that was all. The explosion had blown a large hole in my fur coat (while I was wearing it) and I had no collar. It took about a fortnight to reach Moscow, stopping off at Archangel, and it was a month before I was able to get a respectable suit made. The shops were empty, quite empty, and one needed a special permit to get even basic needs. The suit was lined with green brocade and it was brown, a colour that does not suit me, but it was Hobson's choice. There was no other material. We got our clothes at a department store officially called the Mostorg, but which is still generally called Muir and Mirrlees, from its Scottish owners before the Revolution. We had to go and make ourselves a nuisance every day or they did nothing; at first they hated us, but after a week they loved us and looked forward to our visits. It is always like that. Nothing is done unless you go and badger them continually; the badgerees at first resent being disturbed but, when they get accustomed, they become fond of you.

In a letter home I noted that after a month in Russia I had

also acquired "a nice shirt (price 18s. 6d.), which is only half a size too large, a 6s. hat which is just worth the price, an umbrella (6s. and quite good), six pairs of socks made of paper and cotton mixed, which are wearable but are said to disintegrate in rain, two pairs of tight, shiny black running shorts which do for underclothes, two running vests which are white with blue stripes, and a pair of square-toed black shoes (18s. 6d.) which are quite good value." In place of pyjamas I slept in a long vest lent to me by an American correspondent.

In our long train journey across Russia we had already seen much. We were thrown together with our fellow travellers and for the first time I experienced that feeling of belonging to a Russian crowd. Barriers go down and you feel as if you had all known each other for twenty years. But there were other barriers which did not go down. Beside the railway there was a string of concentration camps in the northern forest, guarded by wooden towers with a vigilant sentry in each, with a loaded rifle in his hand. And at Vologda we saw a very sad group of men and women in dingy clothes sitting on the ground; they were under guard and obviously on their way to exile.

I do not think many people were actually dying of hunger at that time, except in besieged Leningrad, but short of that the shortage was extreme. Ordinary consumer goods had disappeared. If you broke your teapot, you made your tea in a saucepan. One day we saw a queue outside a shop. Clothes-lines were on sale, and that was all, but that was enough to attract a queue. Comparing this with wartime London, it seemed to me as if the war had been going on for twenty-five years with everything running down a little more each year. I had arrived in 1942, which was rock bottom, and there was a great improvement even by 1944, let alone 1968, but traces of the old pattern remain. Things in the shops come and go unaccountably and it is still good policy to join a queue at once without waiting to find what is being sold. If you don't want it, you can always leave the queue, but if you delay you may miss your chance.

My job as Press Attaché was to do wartime publicity and propaganda to the Soviet Union and before going out I had gone round some of the old Moscow hands to get their advice. They were very tactful, but I could see they all thought I was a fool to go. I would not be allowed to meet any Russians and everything I tried to do would be quietly frustrated. I accepted that the work would be difficult, but not that it would be impossible. It seemed impossible to foresee what exactly could be done but I decided to come and look and to take opportunities when they presented themselves. In spite of many setbacks my colleagues and I succeeded beyond even my dreams.

Not long after my arrival Alfred Cholerton, the greatest Moscow correspondent of his day, asked me round to spend the evening with him. I was already beginning to see what the Soviet Union was like, but Chol spared me nothing. We talked on and on, and I began to see that the ramifications of terror and corruption were endless. Innocently I said, "Isn't it strange that the Terror and the Stalin Constitution came together at the same time?" In a flash he answered, "Don't you see? The Terror *was* the Stalin Constitution." While I was trying to think out what depth of hypocrisy or self-deception this betokened, Chol looked me in the eye and said fiercely, "And never forget that there is always idealism."

In my book *Life in Russia* (Allen and Unwin, 1947) I described how Russians lived in the war but said nothing either about my work or about certain people who were still alive. While I was being torpedoed the Ministry of Information had done a deal with the Soviet Government by which we gave them paper and facilities for their wartime propaganda in Britain on condition that they did the same for me in the Soviet Union. So my first and most important task was to organise and edit a British weekly newspaper in Russian, which was by agreement to be uncensored, since Soviet propaganda in Britain was also uncensored. I hardly knew what printer's ink was but, concealing my ignorance, I went straight to Mr. Lozovsky, who was liquidated in the anti-Semitic drive after the war, but was then deputy Foreign Minister in charge of information, and asked him for paper, printers and Soviet collaborators to help us produce our paper. It was to be called the

Britansky Soyuznik or *British Ally*. It came out once a week and was the only periodical published in the Soviet Union, during the war, which was never late. This was a subject of great pride to our Soviet staff and our printers. I told Lozovsky that the *Britansky Soyuznik* would not succeed unless it was useful to them as well as to us; we were all in the war together. He believed me. I received loyal collaboration from the Soviet authorities throughout the war, and I believe they would say the same of me.

The Kremlin was too touchy to accept direct suggestions from their allies but they were open to hints. I would watch what they did and if anything that we did in Britain seemed relevant to their problems, I would publish an article about it. I soon noticed that they had no collection of scrap metal. An enormous iron cylinder, taller than a man and about fifteen feet long, was lying abandoned in one of the main streets of Kuibyshev. So I published an article about scrap collection in Britain. At once the Soviet authorities asked for eight extra copies of the *Britansky Soyuznik* and in about six weeks they started their own campaign for scrap collection, and the cylinder disappeared. Perhaps they would have done the same anyway, though I doubt it, but in any case they could see that we were sensitive to their needs.

Soon the *Britansky Soyuznik* was being read throughout the Soviet Union. We had about half a million readers every week, copies being passed from hand to hand. If we could have got more paper, we should have had millions of readers. The *Britansky Soyuznik* had become a symbol of wartime solidarity with the western allies, a solidarity which aroused many hopes for the future, hopes that, alas! remained unfulfilled.

Since we were uncensored, I had to watch my step all the more carefully. It was obvious that if we made one false step, Stalin would turn on us and the consequences of that would be unpleasant. So I had to find some way of discovering what was going on. Russians have learnt to be more than reserved where foreigners are concerned. The Soviet Press needs expert interpretation and even so it leaves enormous gaps in one's knowledge. So I soon learnt that I must pick up the most important news from tiny hints, but I also learnt that these hints are generally a reliable indication of reality. A silence or a change of subject can be pregnant. Or it can be like those Japanese films when the plot depends on tiny signs. "But surely you saw her hand press the wall?" By nature I am rather unobservant, but in this case responsibility sharpened my faculties. Sometimes I have mis-read the situation but I have made fewer mistakes when I have trusted my own observation of Russia than when I have followed a general view against my own instinct.

It was difficult to get any contact with Soviet citizens and it could not be done quickly; but it was not impossible. It was better not to ask any questions at all and not to refer to any Russian in the presence of any other Russian, unless you had met them both together. No-one would meet you until they were sure you were discreet. But by the end of three years I knew many people, and some of them had become close friends. We had some remarkable meetings. Soon after I arrived, I met the writer Petrov (of Ilf and Petrov) and we *struck ile*. Almost immediately he was killed at the front and very soon after that I met his brother, the equally eminent writer Valentin Katayev, who accepted me as a link with his brother whom he loved. So, we, too, became friends and one day I invited him to lunch in a garden restaurant at Kuibyshev, which was set aside for the diplomatic corps. Lunch was at one but he stayed till eight the next morning; and for the first fifteen hours the conversation was brilliant. In the small hours, when the restaurant closed, we adjourned to the embassy. Evidently this was too much for the N.K.V.D. and Katayev was told to avoid me in future, but one day when I met him in the street with Zoshchenko, it was clear that his feelings had not changed. The quietly sad face of Zoshchenko remains in my mind's eye. I admired his satirical short stories with their penetrating wit and I longed to talk to him, but he was politically under a cloud, and it might have got him into trouble, if he had been seen talking to a foreigner.

I worked hard at my Russian and learnt to speak almost without mistakes, though with a foreign accent, and at the end of two years Russians began to accept me as someone belonging to the country and to talk away in my presence, as if I was not a foreigner. It was then that I learnt how the country really works.

It was a great advantage having a mixed staff of British and Russians, for this meant I talked Russian for at least half the time and that I had to learn how to handle Russians. And, to my surprise, I found the Russians easier to handle than the British. They are more open about their feelings; so you can see trouble coming in the distance and take your measures in time. I found it paid to be very easy-going most of the time but to be uncompromisingly strict when strictness was needed. About once every six weeks I had a blazing row with someone, and that cleared the air. At first I had to spend a great deal of time fighting for better rations for my staff; Soviet rations were graded according to the value of one's work. But later we were able to organise a joint mess where we pooled our more than adequate diplomatic rations with their meagre Soviet rations. In those days no-one taking a job asked what the pay was. They asked, instead, "What do I get?" meaning what perks can you offer in the way of food and clothing and perhaps lodging.

One had to be both ingenious and ruthless to get anything done. Willingness to break the law is normal in Soviet executives; in my position that was out of the question, but I had other cards to play. I give one example of the methods one had to use.

Lozovsky gave us staff, paper, printers' ink and facilities for distribution. What he would not give us was an office outside the embassy. I do not blame him; the congestion at Kuibyshev was fearful; but if we had set up our office in the embassy no-one would have come to see us and we would have been cut off from Soviet life. After puzzling over this, I went to the rat-ridden Kuibyshev hotel and said I was fed up with living at the embassy, and would they give me a room? They were so surprised that they complied. I slept there at night and during the day we moved in chairs and tables and made it into an editorial office. After a bit they became proud that such a distinguished magazine should be published in their hotel and I went back to my more comfortable bed in the embassy. Later, when I wanted more room for our expanded work, I went and sat in the hotel manager's office till he gave me what I wanted. He said I couldn't have it. I said at great length that I must have it. He repeated at equally great length that I couldn't. I repeated my spiel almost word for word. He repeated his. I repeated mine with a smile. He repeated his. I repeated mine, and he began to see that he could do no more work that day, unless he gave me what I wanted. So I got my way, after giving him a free subscription to the *Britansky Soyuznik*, and we parted the best of friends. This is fairly typical of the way things get done in the Soviet Union. It is not so much a question of the smooth carrying out of decrees from on high but of endless arrangements and compromises between those who can bring pressure to bear and those who have something to give. The manager could not turn me out and that gave me a form of pressure that I could bring to bear; and I could do something for him through my control of the coveted *Britansky Soyuznik* (we sold it for one rouble but the second-hand price varied between ten and a hundred roubles, the average being thirty roubles); and who knows whether I might not be able to do him a good turn later on? It was obvious that I had some pull.

For a year I was based on Kuibyshev which struck me as "a badly laid out town in a most beautiful position on the easternmost bend of the Volga with a steep bank this side and lovely green country on the other side. I am amazed at how green everything is. I am writing this letter on a balcony overlooking the Volga with a cool breeze and birds singing and just a few clouds pulled out by the wind into funny shapes, a little like a Perugino sky only paler and more watery." That was in the summer. We used to go on expeditions across the Volga and bathe and walk in the fields and woods. Previously the Russians had taken an absence of bathing dresses calmly, but this was not considered suitable for the wartime capital and an edict had just been issued on this matter. I remember going out in a motor boat with one of the embassy chauffeurs wearing his wife's knickers.

In winter it was hard to believe that it was the same place.

The gentle contours which had grown so familiar were amazingly changed by their dress of snow and ice. I used to skate and ski with more enthusiasm than skill but this made the winter the time when one was fit. When I thought I was beginning to skate better, a tiny little girl shouted out at me, "Uncle! I can skate better than you." But in general it was considered surprising that grown-ups should even try their hand at such sports. Once when I was out on skis with Tom Brimelow—now Sir Thomas, and a Deputy Secretary at the Foreign Office—a little boy called out in surprise, "Look at the boys! But they are not boys. They are uncles." All grown-ups are uncles and aunts to all children in Russia.

On these winter expeditions one had to be careful not to get frost bitten and, when it was very cold, one could neither skate nor ski. On the coldest day I remember at Kuibyshev it was fifty-three degrees of frost (Fahrenheit). But later, at Sverdlovok in the Urals, I experienced seventy-two degrees of frost (Fahrenheit). It was surprising how well one stood this if one kept moving, but if one stood about for even a minute or two out of doors the cold seemed to creep up one's legs and chill one through and through in spite of all furs. On the Volga the frost seemed to have taken all the moisture out of the air and it was very bright and sparkling; a walk across the frozen river and back, which took over an hour, left one pleasantly exhausted like a long day out of doors in a milder climate. A few weeks later it was thawing and I walked across the Volga for the last time "and saw a girl with some pussy-willows, just like at home, but all the willows I saw growing were not even beginning to come out."

These interludes leave a happy memory of Kuibyshev, but most of the time was spent in unremitting work at a pace that only youth can sustain. And the Russians were suffering untold hardships of hunger, cold and overcrowding. From the beginning I tried to spend as much time in Moscow as I could, travelling by trains that might take three days, when one had a two days' ration of food, or by aeroplanes that flew below the tree-tops to escape detection by the enemy. By using all my pull I got

the *Britansky Soyuznik* transferred to Moscow before the rest of
the embassy, which was useful; but it was difficult controlling
an operation that was conducted in two cities several hundred
miles apart in wartime Russia. I heaved a sigh of relief when the
whole diplomatic corps was allowed to return to Moscow, but
I wrote home in August 1943 that "the various material compli-
cations that come out of it all are perfectly hideous. Talk about
Martha; if she had a brother that's me"—evidently I had forgotten the existence of Lazarus—"I spent the whole of today
arguing with the authorities about the food for my Soviet staff;
in the end I have got them the bare minimum for themselves,
but there is not really enough for those with children." That
was before we got our combined mess for British and Russians
on my staff. On Easter Day of the same year I had written, "I
am afraid this has been a hard winter in Moscow. It has not
been cold but fuel has been short and food more so. People in
jobs do not starve, but people who fall out of a job for one
reason or another, may easily come to a grim end. Food is a
little more plentiful in Kuibyshev; and in the countryside on
the whole there seems to be lots to eat, though there is not even
enough paraffin for lamps, so that the peasants have to sit in
the dark. But there are one or two places like Archangel, where
food has to be brought long distances over bad communications"; multitudes were dying of hunger and cold in Leningrad.
"As regards Moscow, things seem to be a bit better now that the
ice on the rivers has melted and things can come in by water."
In the Caucasus in the spring of 1945 I found conditions much
better. Bread was as short as everywhere else, but eggs, cheese,
meat and vegetables were relatively plentiful.

When we moved to Moscow from Kuibyshev, one of the
things that exercised me was how to get some of my staff permission to live in the capital for it was an iron law that no-one
was to come and increase the overcrowding in Moscow unless
he had permission. But I need not have worried. Every train
to Moscow was crowded with people, some of them sitting
on the buffers and some of them lying on the roof. Many of
them had neither tickets for the train nor permission to live in

Moscow, but everything would be arranged. My own staff told me they would live outside and come in every day. At first I was naïve enough to believe this, but I soon discovered that they were sleeping in odd corners of friends' rooms in Moscow.

So Soviet officialdom was not quite what it seemed. At first most of the officials I had to deal with used to put on their official nut-cracker faces when I went to see them. It was no wonder that they were reputed to be inhuman, but by degrees they began to thaw and before the end of three years I saw that some of the reputed toughs were more human than they appeared.

There were many furious political arguments both with officials and with ordinary people. In these the Soviet side always defended their official view with stubborn tenacity, never seeming to give an inch, but one did not know what they thought afterwards when they turned the arguments over in their minds. The fiercest defender of Soviet policy amongst my acquaintances was Ilya Ehrenburg. In his youth he had shown genius as a writer and he would rather have been on the side of the angels but he was not the man to stand out against pressure. He had become Stalin's brilliant hack but, having spent a great part of his life in Paris, his feelings were often more French than Russian. He hated England with the passion of an Anglophobe Frenchman and we had many quarrels. He was a formidable opponent, choosing his ground with great skill and shifting it craftily so that you started arguing about one thing and then found yourself arguing about another without being able to put your finger on how the change had come about. I first met Ehrenburg at the hospitable table of Alexander Werth, now, alas! dead. This was before I knew Russian properly. Ehrenburg and I began a fierce argument in French which went on inter-mittently for more than three years, ending in Russian. I regarded him as thoroughly dishonest and we disliked each other but, for some reason, we were generally seated together at official receptions. One day he turned to me and said, "It is bad luck that they always put us together, when we dislike each other so much." After that I forgave him a lot.

At this time Marxism was at the height of its vogue in the west and I was looking forward to hearing Marxist arguments from the horse's mouth in Russia. But no. So far as I can remember no-one in the course of three years ever tried to expound Marxism to me as a general theory, though many people argued in favour of particular Soviet policies without giving ideological reasons. Marxism had already ceased to be a living force. It had been killed by the purges, by the censorship, which allowed no argument, and by the repeated reinterpretations which had destroyed its credibility as a system of thought.

It seemed at times that even the Communist Party had not really willed the present state of affairs. They had blundered from Revolution into Leninism and from Leninism into Stalinism, without foreseeing the consequences. Such at any rate was the view of one Old Bolshevik whom I got to know well. M. M. Borodin, who had planted Communism in China fifteen years earlier, was still famous, but had fallen into disgrace and was then editing *Moscow News*, the English Language paper published in Moscow. He did this very badly indeed and I said to a Russian friend, "How odd it is that such a very clever man should do his job so abominably badly." "Perhaps it is on purpose," came the reply. His one object was not to attract Stalin's attention, as he might have done if *Moscow News* had been a better paper. Borodin had ceased to be a doer and had become an illusionless spectator of public life. I have often heard him describe how he visited London for a Communist congress in 1907. His eyes would glow as he described the speakers in Hyde Park, but the climax of his story was the speech of welcome that the Prime Minister, Campbell Bannerman, had made. This was true liberty. "You know that is what we all really wanted in 1917." For all his love of Britain he used to say that Glasgow Gaol was the worst prison he had been in, The Tsarist prison at Voronezh being the best. But the story was not yet over. Poor Borodin died after the war in a concentration camp in Siberia, an offering to appease Mao Tse-tung.

Some of the *avant-garde* artists who had put Russia in the front

rank of modern painting earlier in the century were still working, and have now produced a whole school of followers who
have carried their work further, but I heard nothing about
them during the war. Official taste was deadly Philistine, as if
there had been an alliance between the Royal Academy and
the T.U.C. (or the American Federation of Labour) as both of
them were forty years ago. One's friends had often had no
chance of seeing painting later than that of the Edwardian
academics. Many of them had good taste in earlier painting and
the writer Alexis Tolstoy had a good private collection of the
Mannerists of the end of the sixteenth century. But Alexis
Tolstoy was an exception to every rule. He had an extraordinary
face with a shock of black hair like a *moujik*, but a *moujik* whom
someone had placed under a magic spell. I got to know him at
diplomatic receptions where he had an infallible eye for the
bottle with good wine in it. He was a Count, being a distant
relative of Leo Tolstoy, and he had passed many years abroad
between the wars, before he made his peace with Stalin and
returned. He took care to write things that were likely to gain
official approval but he did not go to the lengths that Ehrenburg
went to in order to curry favour. He had a wonderful feeling for
Russian words and for the evolution of the langauge. He was
said to be the only writer who had a proper understanding of
the difference between the Russian of Ivan the Terrible's time
and that of Peter the Great, a hundred and fifty years later. He
and I used to spend hours talking about this kind of thing, but
his feeling for Russian came purely through the ear. He could
not spell and, when he was writing, he used frequently to call
out to his children in the next room, "Children! You devils!
How does one spell . . ." And his children teased him by suggesting absurd spellings. He wrote a play about Ivan the
Terrible, a good play, I thought. Of course it had to be an
indirect glorification of Stalin, but evidently it did not glorify
him enough. There was trouble after the first performance, one
of the complaints being that, when Ivan hit someone, he did not
hit him hard enough. Tolstoy gave tickets for this performance
to me and to my assistant, George Reavey, the poet, but it soon

became obvious that we were not meant to be there. This was a trial run for the Party functionaries, and foreigners were not supposed to be present. Tolstoy introduced us to Pospelov, the editor of *Pravda*, a man with a pale, sour face who made no attempt to conceal his disgust at seeing us. He is one of those who began his rise to power at the height of the Terror in 1937–8 and in 1969 he is still a power for evil.

I met only one man who seemed to understand modern art, Sergey Eisenstein, the great film producer. When the time came for me to leave Moscow he asked me to give him something to remember me by and he chose a print. It was called *The end of a Submarine* but it was really an abstract. A spiral design denoting oil and water seen from the air. When he asked what I would like in exchange I asked for Russian poetry of the period from about 1910 to the early 1920s, which was very hard to get. He came back with an armful of books by Akhmatova, Gumilyov, Mandelstam and the like, and it included a first edition of the *Twelve* by Blok with Annenkov's original drawings. I had indeed exchanged bronze for gold.

Dead as Marxism was, I got no hint of any rival ideology. Religion was scarcely mentioned by educated people, though one could see it had a hold on the simple, and the Russian Orthodox Church had played a great part in rallying doubters to the national resistance. The only person I heard speak of Christianity as a subject of real interest was Boris Pasternak. He was easily roused to enthusiasm and when he got excited I used to think he was like an eagle. He leant forward with his aquiline Jewish features glancing downwards, and bent his arms, working them as if they were wings. Late one evening he suddenly gave us a panorama of world history as he saw it; this could easily have turned into one of his poems but I don't think it did. Lenin had an honourable place in his picture, but it was clear that for Pasternak the Incarnation was the pivot of time and that everything had been changed by the coming of Christ. The best place to see Pasternak was at his *dacha* at Peredelkino near Moscow. He loved the plot of land round his house and it was generally called Neyasnaya Polyana, the Unclear Field, an allusion to the obscurity of his poetry and a contrast with Tolstoy's Yasnaya Polyana, the Clear Field. Pasternak had a game leg but the first time I saw him he was limping more than usual, having just fallen out of an apple tree, which he had been climbing out of lightness of heart on the first day of spring.

Among the intelligentsia Pasternak's interest in Christianity was exceptional, but there was much simple faith among the peasants and workers. National unity was essential during the war. So persecution was halted and religion was tolerated even in the army. One was not supposed to know what happened at Party meetings, but I heard from a good source that the Kuibyshev branch of the Party sent in an official question to the Kremlin asking why religion was being tolerated when it was known to be false. The answer came back that experience showed that a man who had religious faith was likely to be a better soldier.

Writing to my brother in Egypt on 17th September 1942 I described my first and most unexpected encounter with the Russian Orthodox Church, at a time when no Soviet citizens visited foreign embassies except on instructions.

"Yesterday the Metropolitan Nicholas of Kiev and one of his bishops called on us here and were received by the counsellor, Reavey and me. They came in looking like bearded *muzhiks* carrying parcels but in the hall they undid the parcels and dressed themselves up in all their finery which is probably familiar to you from Coptic surroundings but which flabbergasted us. When they went away they undressed again and tucked up their long robes so that they should not show under their coats. It was a touching sight and I felt it was dignified."

It was strictly forbidden to wear clerical dress in the street.

This was the first contact between the Russian Church and the outside world for a long time and it was to have historic consequences. I did not then know how intense the faith of simple people had remained but I had already seen something of the distance that lay between the intelligentsia and any knowledge of Christianity. I quote from an earlier letter to my brother, which describes the very first occasion on which I succeeded in entertaining a Soviet citizen.

"I gave a very nice little girl dinner last night and she was prepared to come to my room and talk, which I enjoyed very much. At one point the following dialogue ensued:

She. (hesitatingly) Do you know that book, the Bible?
Me. Yes.
She. Do you know about Joseph?
Me. Yes, Joseph in Egypt.
She. I've been reading a historical novel about him. (Proceeds to tell me the story of Joseph and his brethren, as if it was the latest novelty.)
Me. Yes, it's a wonderful story. In our country we know all those Bible stories by heart.
She. That is good—they are beautiful stories. But tell me—do you know about Jesus; you know he was first a Jew and then afterwards a Christian?
Me. Yes, he was the founder of Christianity.
She. Yes, that's the man."

CHAPTER III

From Stalin to Brezhnev

I did not visit Russia again for ten years but by 1955 Stalin had been dead long enough for relatively normal relations to be possible. Since then, on every successive visit, I recorded in my diaries a visible improvement in living conditions and a slow but sure tendency towards a more easy-going style of life. But in 1955 the concentration camps were still in full operation and I had no means of knowing that before long the great majority of their inmates would be set free. Nor did I know how very many people I had known in the war had been sent to Siberia or the Arctic by Stalin in the grim last five years of his life. But I knew enough to think it wiser neither to make inquiries nor to attempt to see old friends.

On my next visit, in 1958, all or nearly all of the exiles had come back and Russia was recovering from her wounds. The circulation was returning to numbed limbs though not without pain and difficulty. Soviet citizens were beginning to come on delegations to the west and there had been chances of meeting them often enough to make some new friends but it still seemed better not to try to see anyone one had known before.

In 1959 I visited Russia with my wife, who had never been in the Soviet Union before. It seemed to me that it was now safe enough to try and see some old friends. There are no proper telephone directories in which one can look up the addresses of people one knows; but there is an efficient network of inquiry bureaux housed in kiosks in the streets which answer questions about who lives where, whether he or she has a telephone and how to get there. You pay a few kopeks, get a slip, and return for the answer in about twenty minutes. You do not have to say who you are and you generally get the right answer. As a rule you do not have to stand in a long queue, but you have to guess the age and place of birth of the person you are asking for.

On this visit I was struck by the general improvement in Moscow. My wife was struck by the deficiencies. I wrote in my diary, "An old Moscow hand like myself does not notice the same things as someone on a first visit but Jacynth noticed with horror what the Russians don't have. I noticed with a touch of amazement what they do have, plenty of good food (though there is still a shortage of vegetables), fridges, television sets and good cameras at prices they can afford, etc. The atrociously ugly new blocks of flats make London look like a museum of good architecture and good lay-out, but most families seem to have one or two rooms to themselves, the ghastly cellars in which many people lived are emptying and one does not hear of people sleeping in odd corners, almost like the poorer parts of Asia. For ten years after the war I watched with cynicism the Soviet boasts of their new housing; the published figures showed that the new building was a tiny fraction of what was needed. In the last few years the situation has been transformed, but Moscow's beauty has been destroyed.

"Jacynth notices that people are evasive and avoid certain subjects. I notice that they are prepared to meet one and talk about many things. Jacynth is horrified to find how many people have been in concentration camps. I am pleased to find how many have come back and how few seem to be inside now. Jacynth is maddened by the general inefficiency. I am amazed by the new efficiency of the Moscow telephones. And so on."

We had come in by train from Finland. My wife said, "How extraordinary the change is from Finland to Russia! So slow, but so complete. The woods which were so well kept and the trees so tall and straight have become a tangle of undergrowth, the neat red ochre houses have turned into tumble-down grey houses almost sunk into the ground, in straggling villages. How odd to see women working exactly like men, as porters and even on the line." I noticed the great change from a year earlier when there was a broad front zone left uninhabited for security

3

and it had been heart-breaking to see the undergrowth of fourteen years covering good land. Now cultivation went up to the frontier.

Later my wife wrote, "When I first got here the whole impression that I had seemed to be so oppressive and drab that I wondered if I could bear a week here. It seemed as if a grey dust had settled everywhere and all the people were slightly poisoned. They hurried about as in other capitals but seemed neither to like anything, nor look at anything, nor take any notice of each other. There is an endless stream of people but it seems without purpose. They are either working or not working and that is all. One feels they are never off on some ploy, or going to meet someone, or to rearrange something, or make a fuss as one does in London. But when we went into the cathedral everything changed and there were the Russians I am used to. They were relaxed and at home and their faces full of expression. Hundreds of them packed close together. Among all these lovely glittering lights, and candles and the icons and brilliant coloured carpets and table-cloths with roses and tureens of holy water, and the slow beautiful ritual, they were happy at last." I have heard Russians make similar observations to this last; a young girl said, "When I went into Church I felt that I was myself for the first time in my life"; the intelligentsia sometimes add on going into Church, "So Russia still exists", using Russia's older name *Rus* instead of the modern Rossíya.

On leaving Russia my wife wrote, "After a few days in Moscow I got a little more used to it and it seemed more bearable; there seemed to be cracks in the ice; although from time to time the imprisoning atmosphere overcame me. Indoors it is more relaxed and happier but conversation is very frustrating. They seemed to qualify everything they said. I said to one man what dreadful jobs women have, on the roads, and loading trucks and working on the line. 'Well,' he said, 'they chose their work,' but when I didn't seem satisfied he said, 'No it isn't really women's work.' This happens again and again, until one feels quite confounded. The Russians I know outside the U.S.S.R. are confiding and outspoken and open, and often say *too* much what they think, but here their sense of truth seems damaged and the Russian character spoilt. Moscow does not frighten one. The terror has gone. Of course they lied then. But to lie is quite other than this chaos and lack of direction and indifference to truth which after a time I felt entering my soul. After a time I even found the churches depressing. With all their courage and beauty and wonderful ancient rites, their holy priests and the devotion of the faithful, they seem too still and perfect, as though covered with a golden ice."

All this was acute observation made at a particular moment, and it is part of what I had in mind when I said at the beginning of this chapter that the circulation was returning to numbed limbs not without pain and difficulty. What my wife saw was there to see and what she felt was there to feel. She saw Moscow's Evil Face. A year earlier the monks with whom I visited the Soviet Union had expressed the same thought by telling me that Moscow, though not the rest of the country, was full of devils. This way of putting it will not be convincing to everyone, but there is a palpable power of darkness in Moscow, explain it how you will. This is not the ultimate truth about Moscow, let alone the rest of the Soviet Union, but it is one truth.

In 1959 my wife described the women's clothes on a warm Sunday in June. "The dresses were thin and summery, but very few were made this year. They were shapeless, long and sagging, with uneven hems, they had short sleeves and were tied round the waist. I am sure none of the women wore stays or belt. Skirts and tops were often a different pattern. I didn't see one summer coat. On a chilly day they wore over their dresses a washed up cardigan or the wreck of a jacket of a suit, or at worst—and very commonly—the coat of a man's suit."

On 30th April 1963 I was in Moscow again, and wrote, "Moscow looks more relaxed and the Russians are gradually taking off the mask they wore so long. Manners in the streets are more free and easy. Couples hold hands in public and even put their arms round each other's necks. Uncle Joe would not have stood for that. Where will it end? The girls are much better dressed and are really trying to do something with their hair. I do not wish to exaggerate but some of them might well pass for natives in the less fashionable parts of Wigan."

Eighteen months later, on a winter visit, I found some of the girls wearing smart fur hats and one had a very *with it* piece of wooden costume jewellery in what one might call the Neo-Congolese style. It had been made in Moscow by an amateur. But to return to 1963. "Moscow was already enjoying May Day. That tense feeling that used to go with these Communist festivals had gone, and people seemed to be doing what they wanted and playing about in the streets in a way that was new to me. It used to look as if everything and everybody was part of a cartoon by Giles. Now the people seemed less square and the special Soviet squareness of the lorries and the decorations in red bunting looked out of place."

Two days later I was visiting "the Kazan Railway Station which is a bit of an architectural masterpiece built before the Revolution by the architect of Lenin's tomb in the Neo-Muscovite style. There is an enormous hall with rows and rows of well made wooden benches with backs to lean on, all covered with people waiting patiently for the train to Omsk or Tomsk. They look like peasants from a novel by Tolstoy. Outside a gypsy girl in a tattered grey flannel jacket was begging from a Red Army man. Later I saw a man who looked like a coachman from the time of Pushkin, except that he wasn't wearing a hat; you know the sort of thing, a short striped smock or shirt with a leather belt and that peculiar Russian variant on the theme of Turkish trousers.

"There are so many layers in Russian society. I am fascinated by the *jeunesse dorée* of Moscow. This is something entirely new to me. Last time we stayed at the Moskva, where the spivs make their assignations. This time I am at the dear old Metropole— and ghastly as it is I find I am fond of it. There is a smart new café with an extension on to the street where you see boys and girls looking just like students from Oxford or Cambridge or the L.S.E. There must be some quite good hairdressers in Moscow now, both for men and women. The boys wear summer shirts just like the young in England."

Later on the same visit, in the mountains behind Alma Ata, not far from the Chinese border, groups of boys and girls were going off for the day to scramble in the hills, just like anywhere else. The girls wore slacks or jeans and the boys carried rucksacks and wore clothes like their opposite numbers in western Europe. At that time the girls would not have dared to wear their slacks in the town but it was obvious that a social revolution was on the way. As I wrote up my diary I could hear a dance band such as one might hear in a provincial restaurant in England. I turned on the wireless in my hotel bedroom and it played light music that had no moral uplift at all. Ten years earlier the air would have been filled with patriotic songs and Russian folk tunes.

The progress of the allied causes of jazz and of trousers for women is always a good indication of the degree of social emancipation that the Soviet Union has reached. In 1959 we went to see a French friend who lived near the Canadian Embassy. When the Canadians played jazz records in the summer with their windows open, the Muscovites in nearby flats all got their tape recorders out. Later one could hear the same music coming out of Russian windows with the addition of snatches of other music which the Canadians had played in between. In 1963 Fidel Castro had been visiting the Soviet Union when I was there and I found myself following him round. The next year I did a whirlwind tour of the Soviet Union as an official representative and at every hotel we stayed in there were deafening bands really trying to play modern dance music. Cuba had done much for the freedom to dance.

On a higher level it is instructive to watch the progress of abstract art. In 1959 there had been no improvement in the visual arts. The immense bloated figures, the bad drawing and modelling, the over-emphasis and false sentiment, the screaming glorification of man, the enormous eyes staring into the future and the hands stretching out—to what?—all this was familiar; and it was not even realistic. The only true art my wife and I saw on this visit was the peasant art, clay and wooden toys, models of animals and painted wooden tableware. Some of this was abstract art, which in theory was strictly forbidden, but all "people's" art is specially privileged and the Party was too stupid to see what was happening when sophisticated artists, who wanted to do abstract work, went to work with the peasant craftsmen.

I knew that some of the Russian artists were experimenting with *avant-garde* styles but at first I was not impressed with the little I had seen and I supposed that it was a question of second-rate imitators of the Paris school. Afterwards I found out that this was wrong. It was in 1963 that my friends began to ask me questions about abstract art. Camilla Gray's book, *The Great Experiment*, was known to a few people and indeed it was in Moscow that I first saw a copy of this excellent work, which had alerted some of the Moscow art world to the distinguished part that Russians had played in earlier stages of the development of abstract art. This kindled their interest but they did not find abstracts easy to take. One man was fighting a losing battle against abstraction. It was a nuisance to him, but he was too clever not to see the point, and a few years later he had come right round. Indeed abstract art was making progress every day. Even the attacks were really advertisements. I was taken to see the latest play from Prague at the Sovremennik theatre. The backcloth was an abstract design. Socialist realism demanded that posh flats in Prague should be shown as they are, with abstract designs on the walls, but of course the artist had done his best and in this way the audience were learning to get their eyes accustomed to abstract art. Likewise in the papers one sees drawings attacking abstract art but the drawing usually belies the caption and in this way artists are able to sabotage the Party line without being found out.

In Stalin's day the Kremlin had been a powerful symbol of the aloofness of Soviet rulers. It was like the Forbidden City. During the war I used to look with fascination at its domes from my office in the British Embassy just across the Moscow river but it took a wangle to get inside, even if one had some pull. I first succeeded in this by saying it was my personal duty to deliver a ghastly picture of the signing of the Anglo-Soviet treaty by the late Frank Salisbury. I sat in the lorry with this enormous picture, submitted to a strict security check and had my first close look at those amazing domes and pinnacles. In 1959 one could stroll freely in and out of the Kremlin walls, though certain buildings were strictly cordoned off. The churches have become museums, but the sanctuary is shut off and one is not allowed inside it. People generally behave decorously but once I saw three young workmen striding through the Uspensky Sobor wearing their caps. I called out sharply, "Comrades, take your hats off! That's not polite." I had to repeat myself, but they obeyed. Once I tried to visit the same church when it was having its weekly clean. Girls in overalls were sweeping vigorously and climbing up ladders. I made friends with the custodian and thought he would let me in, but he said firmly, "It wouldn't be proper," and he pointed to the girls on ladders and said, "They drive even me out." I had forgotten that unsophisticated Russian women wear no underclothes.

I used to think that the old Russian art of living had been killed by the Revolution, but in 1964 I saw signs of a revival. I remember specially a dinner in a flat in a southern Russian town. The *chef-d'œuvre* was a home-made cake, a splendid work of art based on thin slices of black bread, fresh fruit and lots of cream. Since then I have met that cake again. On this occasion the excellent wine came from vines in our host's *dacha*, and his wife had added herbs to the vodka to give it special flavouring. Our hostess had all the virtues of a first-class, old-fashioned Russian housekeeper, her husband being one of the artistic leaders of an important modern city.

Meals remain erratic in both time and quality. Sometimes you sit down to two enormous meals in immediate succession. One day I got nothing to eat till two forty-five and nothing at all after that. So I ate a very large meal and soon afterwards began to feel sorry for the boa constrictors.

Increasingly, as the years go by and the opportunities increase, people embellish their private lives with comfort and beauty but the public authorities sometimes set a bad example.

In a leading Moscow hotel there was a big Azerbaijani party one night in 1959 and some debris was left. The next morning I saw some men and women cleaning the parquet floor; some were waiters, others were dressed like Victorian housemaids, and others were old women wrapped in nondescript bundles of clothes. Most of them had bare feet. First they sloshed buckets of water till it stood in pools on the parquet, then they scrubbed it with lumps of soap and scrubbing brushes till it made a sort of mud pie. Then they put an electric polisher into the middle of the mess. No doubt they were doing what they were told to do and no doubt it would have been useless for them to argue. It may well have been laid down in the plan that soap, water and electric polishers should all be used; but in their own homes they would have behaved more sensibly.

There are many times when the muddle and not caring get one down, and for many people these experiences reach a climax in the Astoria at Leningrad which has the makings of a good old-fashioned hotel. One morning in 1959 my wife and I arrived there after a night journey. Intourist had made us pay for an expensive room though we were not spending the night, but when we arrived they said we had no right to a room. I got angry and shouted but they told us to wait in the hall for an hour and a half till the boss arrived. So I got still more angry and we were at once given the Rajah's suite. I knew I should get my way in the end but it took two exhausting hours. The suite had a bedroom, a dining-room, a drawing-room, a study, a hall, a bathroom, and a lavatory. We valued the furniture and fittings as at least fifteen hundred pounds by 1959 London prices—say five thousand dollars. On the housemaids' table outside the door was, and no doubt still is, an Empire ormolu lamp of the finest quality worth at least a hundred pounds (or about three hundred dollars) ten years ago.

During our wait we had breakfast in the restaurant. All the bits were brought higgledy-piggledly, here an omelette and there a pat of butter. When we asked for something to fit what had been brought, the waiter whispered in my ear, "We have no trays." At the next table were four charming Indian artists headed by Professor M. S. Sundaram from India House in London. They thought it all as funny as we did and I felt like saying, "How wonderful to meet fellow-Europeans again! At last another white man!"

In reality the Russians are very European, though a special kind of European, but they have been so cut off from the life of Europe for so long that they do not know where they are. I sometimes feel that they are groping their way back to where they were fifty years ago, in their culture, I mean, not in their social structure. At any rate there is a special interest in some of the writers of the earlier part of this century. In 1958 a foreigner who had lived in Moscow for many years told me that he had asked "all his friends" whether they would rather have a house of their own, or a chance of travelling abroad every year. A house was a very valuable thing to a Soviet citizen, but every one of them said he would rather have the chance to travel. My friend confirmed my impression that the Russians were already living in a spiritual vacuum. The Party was no longer able to find new recruits with any ideological fervour. So it contented itself with recruiting any keen young men or women who did their jobs well and accepted socialism in a general way without asking awkward questions.

In 1959 my wife and I travelled by boat from London to Leningrad, being served with rice pudding and caviare for breakfast every day. About half the passengers were Soviet citizens and they included some D.P.s on their way home. One was a Latvian who spoke a mixture of bad English, bad German and gibberish, and said he had forgotten his native Latvian. He was going home to a wife and daughter, whom he had not seen for fifteen years. One man at our table looked terrified and never spoke, but once he smiled at me and I discovered that he was going to Stalingrad which he had left in 1941. Then after three or four more days the other Russians evidently convinced him that things really had changed since Stalin died and he began to look quite happy. On this boat one saw a good side of Soviet life. Even four years before one could tell the Soviet citizens from others by something furtive in their behaviour, quite apart from their clothes. Now this particular lot had bought their clothes in London and there was loud, uninhibited backchat between ship and shore as we left Surrey Docks seen off by some of the Soviet colony in London. The various national groups on the boat tended to stick together but the Russians did not mix less than the rest. They seemed classless, not middleclass and not working-class but something new. They were unselfconscious about class and this seemed to infect the Scandinavian passengers who took on the same classless atmosphere. The British, however, carried vestiges of snobbery with them. Later in Moscow a real live prince was pointed out to us in a restaurant, not I think out of snobbery but as a curiosity. He had been an émigré but had recently returned and was making a career in Moscow.

At this time curiosity about foreign countries was just beginning to be less inhibited. Two cheerful young workmen from the Likhachev factory slightly emboldened by drink, got into conversation with us in the street and asked, "Is it true that the workers have a hard time in England?" I answered, "It is no longer true," and they said to each other, "You see it is just stories." This was the phase described by my wife earlier in this chapter when the Russians were beginning to ask aloud questions that not long before they had scarcely dared to ask in their hearts. On the Korean war they would stoutly maintain the official line but some of them knew what they had done in Hungary and admitted this privately.

Four years later doubts were spreading. A young Russian whom I met in 1963 in a *chai khaneh*, or tea house, in Tadjikistan argued obstinately until in irritation I said, "I see you are always right." Then he blushed and came right off it. "But don't you think it is wrong to spy? What about Greville Wynne?" Mr. Wynne was at that moment being tried in Moscow for espionage. I said with a grin that I wasn't really up in spying and I didn't like it, yet that all countries spied. "We catch yours from time to time." He gasped with surprise but did not dispute this unexpected information. The awful feeling was growing among Russians that sometimes foreigners knew more about what the Soviet government is doing than they knew themselves.

A year later, just after the fall of Khrushchev, the old cockiness had quite gone. When we were by ourselves an official contact asked, quite simply, "Who started the cold war? — You or we?" I answered that on the whole they started it, though we were not entirely free from blame. This seemed to be accepted. From this time the way in which one's superior foreign knowledge was accepted became rather touching. During the fall of Khrushchev the Russians had got most of their foreign news from the B.B.C's Russian service, which I had had a hand in starting in 1941, just before the Russian period of my life began. In one provincial town the wireless of the official car which drove us round was permanently plugged in to the B.B.C's home service; I remember a concert of Irish songs broadcast from Nottingham town hall, as well as news bulletins of course. The Voice of America, Radio Liberty and other foreign stations have their listeners, but not so many as the B.B.C.

The reaction to Khrushchev's fall was general satisfaction combined with widespread resentment at the way in which it had been engineered. Two or three years earlier one used to hear, "It is all right under Khrushchev, but God knows what will happen when he goes." Now the Russians seemed sure that the danger of a Stalinist reaction was over and they felt that Khrushchev was a brake on further progress. Events showed, however, that this prognosis was too sanguine.

Yet the new government of Brezhnev and Kosygin had a cold welcome. One might think that the Russians would be hardened to having their rulers changed over their heads; but this was too much, or rather it was too late. In Stalin's day the Russians were numbed with fear, so that they never discussed changes among their rulers and hardly thought about them, except as a sailor thinks about the clouds in order to discern what is coming next. But they were beginning to recover and they expected at least to be told why the government had been changed. If the conspirators who overthrew Khrushchev had given the people a consistent reason for their action and given it promptly, they could have gained the respect of their subjects without too much difficulty, but they missed the moment for that.

The Russians are very patriotic and the increased coming and going with foreign countries and the new liberty to listen to unjammed foreign broadcasts were making them more aware of their national rating in the world. They were beginning to suspect that while their national achievements were universally respected, some of the ways of their rulers were despised as neo-barbarian. This was galling to their intense national pride and the Communist Party had lost caste with the Russian people. The consequent insecurity of Khrushchev's successors has led them into fumbling reaction. At the end of 1964, however, optimism still prevailed, and people were looking forward to a more easy-going time to come. A film by Yury Nagibin about collective farms called *The Chairman* was nearly ready for release and "It hides nothing, absolutely nothing." It was shown for a short time and then withdrawn. Another film about the life of Andrey Ryublyov, the great religious painter of the fifteenth century was well on the way and its release was confidently expected. Four years later we are still waiting for it.

Not long after the end of the war I had become convinced, to my considerable surprise, that the Christian religion was true. And, if true, it was important. So in the years since my visit in 1955 I have seen a good deal of the Russian Church, and I have observed the changing attitude to religion of both government and intelligentsia. Simple people have not changed much in their attitude. Many believed and many did not. In neither case were they greatly influenced by the views of educated people or of the government, though in times of per-secution the practise of religion might be difficult or impossible. Belief, however, where there was belief, survived the closing of churches.

In Russia religion is tied up with patriotism in a way that is both good and bad. Even atheists are sure that the Russian Orthodox Church is the best Church. And there is a surpris-ingly widespread view—which is I believe true, however

strange it may seem — that the Church of England is the nearest
to Orthodoxy of all the foreign Churches. Even in the eyes of
the atheists this is one up for *Anglikanstvo*.

In 1958 the Church was still enjoying the relative peace won
by her patriotism in the war. The savage persecution of the first
twenty years of Bolshevism was past, and the renewed persecution of the nineteen-sixties had not begun. On arrival I
asked a church friend how the Russian Church had been
getting on. He answered, "Since you were last here three years
ago, the young people have been coming to us more and more."
When I asked some supplementary questions, he smiled and
said, "You will see for yourself." I did. The very young were
not much seen in church but there were many of the young
married. The fact that the Church was winning an important
section of the younger generation was the chief cause of the
renewed persecution that was being prepared even then,
though I did not know it. In a Leningrad church I saw a queue
of mothers having their babies christened. I asked how many
christenings there were that day. "Only about a hundred and
eighty. You see it is an ordinary weekday." "How many babies
would be christened on a Sunday?" "Oh, about three hundred,
but in some churches as few as two hundred." These figures are
affected by the small number of churches which are allowed to
be open but other evidence indicates that even so the baptism
of babies was almost universal at that time. However, a few
years later baptisms in the same church were to be reckoned
by scores instead of hundreds. Those parents whose children
were known to be baptised risked various forms of unpleasant-
ness, such as losing their jobs, and it was forbidden for baptisms
to take place without the written consent of both parents, which
could be brought up in evidence against them for ever afterwards. Of course some baptisms take place on the quiet but
there is no means of knowing how many of these there are.

Even in the nineteen-fifties the only way, apart from private
conversations, in which religious teaching could be given was by
sermons and these had to be very carefully phrased if they
touched on dangerous ground. Once I heard a very effective

sermon on the man born blind. The preacher spoke of the unbelief of the Pharisees in a way which was a covert answer to the official propaganda about miracles, but it was done so delicately that no-one could take exception. The concluding words were, "Let us not be like the Pharisees. Let us not think that we who come to church are better than those outside. At the last judgment they may be placed on the right and we on the left."

The Church makes no overt comment on public affairs, except to support the Party line on "peace" and allied matters, but after the 1958 Lambeth Conference I was interested to find a lively off-the-record interest in the Conference's resolutions on such subjects as the family in the modern world, race relations and the atom bomb. A leading churchman from the Soviet Union, whom I met stark naked in a Finnish sauna, told me that there were two great temptations for a Church living under Communist rule. One was to become bitter and the other was to retire from the world into a pietistic huddle.

One day my wife and I lunched with the late Fr. Ruzhitsky, the Rector of the Theological Academy in the great monastery of St. Sergius near Moscow. He was a very clean and neat old gentleman with beautiful silver hair coming down to his collar. He kissed me affectionately and we sat down to a very slow meal. The only other person present was an ex-seminarian who was very much on his good behaviour. The Rector looked hard at him when the conversation turned to seminary discipline and smoking was mentioned. After lunch the young man admitted to us that he had been one of the offenders. While we were seeing the sights he amused himself by trying to catch the pigeons with corn, in which he eventually succeeded; the pigeon was not frightened. He had had eight years at the seminary and had got thoroughly fed up with it.

Russian priests have to be married, unless they are monks, and at lunch the conversation turned to priests' wives. The wives of ordinands were always seen first by the parish priest and sometimes chosen by the Church. To be a priest's wife was a dedication. Nearly all the marriages were happy. Even the wives who at first seemed unsuitable generally turned out well. Fr. Ruzhitsky asked one girl who was sent to him why she wanted to marry a priest. She answered, "A priest can only marry once." This led on to divorce, and he explained that when there is a broken marriage the Church distinguishes between the innocent and the guilty parties; but even the guilty party will be received back into communion, if he or she repents, even if there is a second marriage.

Fr. Ruzhitsky spoke a good deal about his wife and family. In a few days, he and his wife were due to go to their house just outside Kiev. He had a large garden with two magnificent fir trees, two limes and more than a hundred fruit trees. He kept his private car at Kiev for holiday times; he got thirty-nine days of holiday in the summer when he could go to his beloved Ukraine. He missed the southern liveliness, and regarded central Russia as almost a place of exile.

He said, "A priest who is on good terms with his flock lives well and has no need to buy clothes; he gets given everything, including a magnificent cross or crucifix every year and sometimes cocks and hens as well." He did not say that the faithful love their priests because they know what they have been through. Nor did he say how hard life can be for a priest's wife and family if his licence to officiate is withdrawn by the government, and how hard it can be for him to get other work when he has this blot on his official record. Most stand firm but some give in to a pressure that can be very severe. In the nineteen-sixties it has been sad to see the deterioration of some of those who showed great promise in the 'fifties. The judgment of the Book of Revelation on the seven Churches that are in Asia reads like a contemporary document, if one knows the Russian Churches' conditions of life.

When I visited Russia in 1963 and 1964 the renewed persecution was already under way and one had to be very discreet. I asked no awkward questions but I knew already from other sources that about half the too few churches open in the nineteen-fifties had been closed. And other closures were to come. On the other hand the revival of intellectual interest in religion was in preparation. I was not able to foresee the remarkable development of the next few years but enough was happening to prepare one for the change that was soon to come. The B.B.C's Russian service had broadcast both sides of the controversy about the Bishop of Woolwich's book *Honest to God* and this had started a theological discussion in which both believers and unbelievers had taken part. Makartsev, the number two at the Ministry of Cults, expressed it by saying that he heard some Bishop had proved there is no God. I said it was not quite like that and we had quite a good argument.

One morning I was accompanied to church by a very intelligent woman. She expressed delight at the music but indifference to everything else. However, she could not leave the subject alone, and returned to it when we went to the opera that evening. I had become a believer when I was nearly forty, whereas she had been brought up religious and had gone right away from the Church. How come? "I found it was not possible to live any other way." "How should one live?" After this we had a conversation about how to live, like something out of a Russian novel, except that it was carried on in snatches in an undertone, largely in the intervals between acts. "I think a man ought to stand on his own feet." "That's nonsense." Conversation interrupted by the orchestra.

Later we shared a convivial meal with other friends and someone else tackled me at once about religion. I questioned something he said about the course of events in Russia and added that people like him had been so far from the Church for so long that they did not know what had happened. This seemed to be generally accepted. "What does youth think about religion in Britain?" "There are a good many believers and a great many seekers and doubters but not many downright atheists." This last point caused astonishment but there was no wish to argue. Then my friend of earlier in the day had her chance. "How can one believe when there is so much suffering in the world?" I paused and said it was easy to give a superficial answer, and then I said, "That is the Cross." She started crying but would not leave the subject alone, so I said, "The one thing God will not do is to take our freedom from us." The tears then became uncontrollable and she covered up by saying we had been talking about the war and she could not bear it. So I helped her out by giving a boring diatribe about my own experience of the war in Russia. Then we turned to some highly intellectual and neutral subject. When we said goodbye she did not look me in the eye. A few years later a Jewish leader of a Soviet group visiting Britain asked me a similar question about religion in Britain. I answered, "There are a good many believers and very many seekers, but only a few convinced atheists." Evidently that was the answer he was expecting. This reflected a change in Soviet society. One never knows what people think secretly, but for a long time the appearance of dogmatic atheism had been usual. Now this was no longer so.

CHAPTER IV

Monasteries and Pilgrimages

In 1958, by one of those coincidences that some people take to be more than coincidences, I had an unusual opportunity to see the insides of a number of Russian monasteries with a group of Anglican monks. This was the first delegation of its kind, and so far the only one. It takes a matter of years to organise a visit of this sort and to get the agreement of the Soviet authorities. I had been consulted about the monks' plan from the beginning, but there was no idea that I should accompany them. However, I found myself travelling to Moscow by the same plane as they. I was booked as a tourist but I was more than ready to scrap my plans if I could see the monasteries with them. So I had asked them to write to the Moscow Patriarchate saying that we would arrive together and expressing a hope that I might accompany them for part of the time. It was not known till we arrived late at night whether this suggestion was acceptable, but I was received most hospitably in the general embrace and for a fortnight I almost became a monk myself, visiting religious houses in the company of Russians and English for whom the cloister was the air they breathed.

Before that, however, we were taken off and given a large banquet of sturgeon and caviare, though it was well past midnight. A private dining-room in the Metropole Hotel was set aside for us whenever we were in Moscow. The next morning we were received by the Patriarch, who was already an octogenarian, at the Monastery of St. Sergius at Zagorsk, fifty miles from Moscow. Father Mark Gibbard of the Cowley Fathers, who was the leader of our delegation, had prepared what we thought was a suitable little speech. I was to translate it into Russian but his Beatitude after listening for a short time, at the first break in Fr. Gibbard's flow, said "Amen". That was that, we were escorted into a neighbouring room and given tea. The only people present were ourselves, the Patriarch, his interpreter, Fr. Pimen the *Namestnik* or Abbot of the Monastery, and the famous Metropolitan Nicholas,* who had long been the Patriarch's right-hand man. I had already known him for sixteen years on and off and I viewed him with some suspicion, though I did not feel the extreme distrust that was professed by some observers. On this occasion the conversation was very informal and I saw a warmer side of his personality. Subsequent events led me to believe that my suspicion of the Metropolitan Nicholas had been unjust. A few years later he died in circumstances that have never been satisfactorily cleared up and is now generally regarded as a confessor of the faith, and by some as a martyr. I remember him as a man of medium height with a trim grey beard and with a twinkle in his eye. He had a gift of throwing himself into any situation and was cast in the mould of some of our Tudor or Renaissance bishops. Like them he could survive in a dangerous world of political intrigue and, like some of them, he had, in spite of all, a lively faith and a gift of eloquence that almost made him a great preacher.

During the 'twenties and 'thirties organised monastic life was stamped out, but for various reasons and in various ways the war had brought a revival. At this time there were about eighty religious houses in Russia with about five thousand monks and nuns, three-quarters of them being nuns. One of the greatest monasteries was that of St. Sergius where our meeting with the Patriarch took place. This place is hallowed by patriotic memories of times when the monks stood to the walls to resist Polish invaders and organised the national resistance at a dark hour in the seventeenth century. And St. Sergius himself, a very great and very Russian saint, is also a symbol of Russian patriotism. I had first seen the monastery of Zagorsk during the war. If any brave old monks were still living in the monastery, perhaps in cells somewhere in the fortified walls, they kept quiet. The ancient buildings with their star-spangled onion

* It was he who had visited us at the British Embassy in 1942 (see chapter II).

domes were well looked after but they were empty and all the beauty seemed as chilly as the grave. Now there was a quiet life and warmth. We had silent meals in the refectory while a monk read from the lives of the saints in Old Slavonic; I could not understand it and I am sure that most of the monks couldn't either. The food at this and other monasteries was adequate but rather simple and I gathered that most monks have a bit of extra food in their cells. On special days we were given kvass, a most refreshing drink made from slightly fermented black bread with fruit juice. Monastery kvass is famous, and it deserves to be, but kvass must be just right or it becomes acid and is barely drinkable.

The Abbot, who was our intimate companion for ten days, represented the new type of Church leader who was then coming to the fore. Now a bishop, he was then in his thirties. Tall and distinguished, gay and perceptive, with a quick eye for human realities, he had passed his whole life under Soviet rule. He had a contemporary mind and saw life as it must be lived today, but one could never forget that he sees this world against a background of eternity. The waitress at the Metropole who looked after us thought it a great waste that he was not married. In the generation that both he and she belonged to there are too few men and too many women, owing to the war. In the monastery he had a reputation for strict discipline, but I doubt whether he has by nature quite the toughness and stamina which is necessary for leadership in Soviet life, in the Church no less than the world. In the monastery he had two assistants: a *starets* or elder, and a monk who was bursar, steward and workmaster. The bursar was young and had been a lorry driver in Astrakhan before he became a monk. If you ask what a *starets* is, the best answer is to say that Father Zosima in The Brothers Karamazov is a *starets*; he holds no office of authority and is appointed by no-one, but is recognised as a man of God. His influence can be enormous.

Beside the quiet life of the monks and the theological college and academy housed in the monastery, there was another life of tourists and pilgrims who came to pray at the shrine of St.

Sergius. In addition to the usual Liturgies and other monastic services, there is a steady stream of *akathists* all day. This is a liturgical service peculiar to the eastern Church and these particular *akathists* are in honour of St. Sergius who is loved in this region in the way that St. Columba is loved in Donegal, not as a distant historical figure but as a friend who is beside them now. An unbroken chain of prayer goes on from five o'clock in the morning till eight o'clock in the evening. The monks start singing the service but, when there is enough congregation, one of the women taps a monk on the shoulder, the monks go away, and the congregation take over. One of the women holds a very large book with the service written out in Church Slavonic, she leads the singing and the others join in. The chants suddenly become more like Russian folk tunes and one is caught up in a new way. Those who do not know the service stand behind and read the book. The writing is so large that I have found one can read it from about twelve feet away, provided that you know the Slavonic alphabet, which is an earlier form of the present Russian alphabet. And surprisingly many people do know it. After an *akathist* is finished there is a rhythmical singing of "Lord have mercy" for several minutes and then another *akathist* begins.

The fervour and recollection of these peasant and working-class congregations is a force that has to be felt to be understood but their faith sometimes has quaint expressions. One day an old woman came up to me and said, "Our Lord would not allow himself to be photographed." "But Babushka, in our Lord's day there were no photographers." "Oh yes there were. This is the origin of all the icons of the Saviour. The Tsar (Caesar) sent messengers to the Saviour, saying 'Please send me your photograph', but the Saviour refused and, instead, he took out his handkerchief and wiped his face with it. His features left a mark upon the handkerchief and he sent it to the Tsar. This is the origin of all the icons of the Saviour." At this point a modern young man from the Moscow Patriarchate interrupted and said, "Babushka, those are fairy tales," at which the old woman became indignant. I thought of the legend of St. Veronica.

Ten years later I was at Zagorsk for the Falling Asleep of the Blessed Virgin Mary which is the festival that corresponds with the Assumption in the Catholic Church. I arrived about nine a.m. by train from Moscow and tried to get into the church of the theological academy but I was late and could not even get on to the stairs; people standing in the garden joined in the Our Father, which came floating out of the window. However, I was in time for the late liturgy at the big church. It was crowded and sweat poured down, but it was impossible to take my jacket off. There was hardly room to make the sign of the cross. At the end there was an ugly rush to kiss the cross and I was pushed against some women, who reproached me for it. "But the crowd pushes." They answered severely, "A man ought to stand firm." Outside, people were relaxing quietly on benches or on the grass, eating picnics, gossiping or going to sleep.

A good deal of bench space was taken up by peasant women stretched out asleep, sometimes with other people perched on the edge of the bench and almost crushing them. One of the group was listening to a woman with a strong face who was reading aloud in a firm voice. When I stopped for a minute, they made room for me to sit down. I was fascinated but, after my early start, I fell asleep. When I awoke the woman was still reading and still holding her audience. She was uneducated and read firmly, but with some hesitation, from a notebook.

It was the poor man's *Dream of Gerontius*, an account of what happens to the soul for the first forty days after death. You go up a sort of Jacob's Ladder with your guardian angel and on every rung there is a platform where devils assail you. Your guardian recounts your good deeds and if there are enough of them, you go on to the next rung. The last rung is the most dangerous and few get by it, for there you are called to account for all your "fleshly desires". The hearers wanted to be sure they had understood that right, and when it was explained there were some knowing nods. Then there was a long description of the way in which Satan tempts men and women, both sexes equally. And after that there was a rather touching account of the soul's meeting with the Lord and with people it has known on earth "who will all be called by their names".

Later the document tailed off with a lot about ritual acts, the sin of talking in church and the importance of making the sign of the cross properly. "Don't do it like this, as if you were thinking of something else," and the reader moved her hands rapidly in a narrow orbit, "but like this." And she sat upright with an air of deep concentration and moved her hand slowly up and down, right and left, with three fingers together in the Orthodox way, in a generous movement that went to the full breadth of her shoulders.

All this comes from a very old layer of Russian folk religion which I had read about but never expected to see. The rungs of the ladder were the "heavenly customs posts" of the Russian middle ages. The document described itself as an *Epistoliya* and claimed to have been miraculously revealed to the Patriarch of Jerusalem. Great benefits were promised to those who copied it, those who read it, and those who heard it. If we did not mend our ways another *Epistoliya* would follow. The women listened attentively to the end but there was no discussion and very little comment. One woman said, "We don't really know what heaven and hell are but we know that we are all sinners." Another said, "We know the most important thing is to pray for those who have fallen asleep" (namely the dead).

Nearly everyone had brought a receptacle, generally an aluminium milk can, to get some cool, clear water from the holy well discovered by St. Sergius, and there was a long queue for the water. I was longing for some, because the only other drinks were *portvein* and that horrid fizzy lemonade; but I had no receptacle.

The monks and I went down to Kiev and visited the famous monastery of the caves, the oldest religious house in Russia, which has since been closed, but this has been described often enough in other books. We also visited two convents. One occupied a dignified building* and we were told with awe that the Patriarch's sister had been a nun there. The nuns

---

* As I write news comes that this convent is threatened with closure.

seemed to be highly educated, to come from families of some position, and to be well accustomed to receiving visitors. This convent evidently had a high position in society. The other convent was lodged in some ramshackle buildings at the other end of the town and it was obvious that visitors were a rarity. The nuns were simple peasant girls, speaking the earthy language of the Russian countryside which sounds so strange in Russian-novel-English, with its "little mothers" and "little pigeons".

From the moment we arrived one of the chief local priests was determined that we should all go in speed-boats on the Dnieper. He succeeded in persuading everyone that this was desirable, so we found ourselves racing up and down the river. This priest stood in the prow of the boat, with his monastic robes streaming out behind and encouraging the driver to ever wilder and wilder feats, until his robes got caught up in the engine. After this that particular boat went slightly more carefully.

Later at Odessa we visited a convent that was quite different again. The nuns were gay, practical and active and they operated an efficient flour mill with modern machinery. They crossed themselves as they turned on the machinery and then ran with sacks to the place where the flour would pour out of wide mouths of burnished copper. At that time they supplied communion bread for the diocese but most of the monasteries and convents, including this one, have since been closed by the government. In the 'fifties the officials in charge of Church relations were often on good terms with the Church, and the Odessa representative of the Council for the Affairs of the Orthodox Church seized me by the arm saying, "How can one say that it is only old people who go into monasteries? Look at those girls. They can't be more than seventeen or eighteen." Many were indeed young, but the Abbess was aged and simple and had been a nun since she was ten. In all the Russian religious houses we saw radiantly beautiful faces but I remember the faces here better than any.

In Odessa we stayed in the monastery which is sometimes described as the Patriarch's *dacha* or country cottage. It is in fact a full-sized monastery, standing in its own ground by the sea, some miles from Odessa. This is black earth country and the monastery has a very fertile and well-kept garden. When the Patriarch is here he stays in a largish separate building in the monastery grounds; a year or two before our visit a large two-storied veranda had been built onto it; this was almost completely surrounded with glass, some of it coloured, and had a fine view towards the sea.

The monastery stands at the top of a two hundred foot cliff. We descended by the funicular railway which was built for a former Patriarch and found a smart Soviet policeman guarding the Patriarch's private beach. There was a small wooden pier sticking out about thirty feet into the sea with a large, rather elaborate, Victorian bathing booth at the end, for the Patriarch to bathe from. Twenty yards to the left was another and smaller pier and a smaller bathing booth for the Archbishop of Odessa to bathe from; we were given the free run of this, the water was warm and hardly salty at all, since the rivers Dnieper and Bug flow into the sea not far away and in the spring their waters sweep along the coast, keeping it fresh for many tens of miles. The Russian monks bathed with us, exchanging their long robes for bathing drawers, but their long hair caused them some difficulty. One plaited it into two pigtails, another made it into a bun and the young Abbot did it into a horse's tail. Unfortunately photography is forbidden on the seashore.

The Abbot, who was only twenty-five, suffered from what is a great misfortune to a Russian clergyman; he was unable to grow a proper beard and his face was covered with irregular tufts. He always carried a ciné camera slung outside his robes. He was an only son and, his father being dead, his mother had become a nun and was nominally attached to the convent in Odessa but in fact spent most of her time at the men's monastery looking after her son, who told me that, as I might imagine, he could not have a better *keleinik* (a sort of monastic batman).

After a very long, very early and very wonderful service we breakfasted with the Archbishop, whose *residentsiya* was a spacious villa with a largish garden on the outskirts of Odessa.

A sumptuous meal was served under a large canopy surrounded by flowering shrubs. This patriarchal scene conveyed vividly the important position occupied by at least some of the Russian bishops at that time. The late Archbishop Boris was an impressive personality but the fact that he came to high office without any known church background has cast some doubt on his motives.

Ten years later I visited another of the great Russian monasteries, this time by myself. The Lavra of the Caves near Pskov is the only one of the Russian monasteries of the first rank where the monastic life has been lived continuously and without hindrance throughout Soviet times. The Lavra was just over the border in Esthonia and so escaped the Soviet repression of religion in the 'twenties and 'thirties. It lies in a steep hollow two or three hundred yards across and almost entirely surrounded by hills about a hundred and fifty feet high, crowned by a stout fortified wall, which the monks have recently restored to its original form by their own labour with the help of technical advice from the state. Inside the hollow are churches and other monastic buildings from the sixteenth century to the first part of the nineteenth century, all in beautiful repair. The domes are painted a deep blue, spangled with golden stars, all the gilt being proper water gilding, as indeed is usual in Russia. The Lavra was in equal degrees a fortified strong-post of very considerable importance and a renowned holy place. Hermits settled here in the dense woods about the fourteenth century, and the place became a regular monastery in the fifteenth century. Soon after, the Tsars placed a permanent garrison there; and they, with the monks, had to defend the walls against many attacks from Swedes, Germans and Poles.

I went into the church of the Dormition, a low, vaulted, rambling building with icons in eighteenth-century gilt frames. The chief icon was by Aleksy Maly, who was a monk here in the sixteenth century. On the other principal wall is an icon by the present Abbot, who was a professional artist before he became a monk. An *akathist* was in process and I forgot about time. The chapel was not large but all Russia seemed to be there. Women of all ages, cripples, even a holy fool, like the man in *Boris Godunov* who has his penny taken away, some men, mostly young, some obviously from the intelligentsia, one young man with long hair and beard and an intelligent face was presumably a priest, though he was wearing ordinary clothes. The people joined in the singing, not very tunefully but from the heart, and we were carried away.

Then they started dishing out water from a holy spring. There were three large enamel buckets and a grey-haired woman with a strict face and an unfashionably long skirt and a long jacket stood with a saucepan ladling it into bottles, jugs and aluminium containers with lids. An old priest dipped a large whisk into the water and went round sprinkling us all methodically, not just a few drops as in the Catholic *asperges*, but a regular soaking so that afterwards one of the monks exclaimed at the wetness of my jacket.

The monastery takes its name from the wonderful natural caves in the soft sandstone. The air is always dry and the temperature is constant at five degrees centigrade. The monks did not say so but it is widely believed that some of the bodies buried here have never corrupted. So for centuries this has been a favourite burying place, and some of the burials from the seventeenth and eighteenth centuries are marked by very pretty ceramic plaques. I saw the resting places of some canonised saints and of more than one *starets* recently dead who is revered as a saint and may be canonised one day. From conversations in Pskov I gathered that certain of the monks have a great reputation for holy wisdom.

Above the caves there is a lovely secret garden reaching up to the walls behind the churches, planted with trees of immemorial age, and crowned with a little pavilion where Peter the Great used to go and smoke, when the monks wouldn't let him smoke anywhere else.

Forty monks are needed as a minimum to do the monastery's essential work but there are eighty monks there now, besides six or seven aged nuns who live in the grounds. There are always also some students from the theological colleges and from other colleges, who come for a time to share the life of the monks, so that the total community is over a hundred. When I was there, monks and students were reconstructing the ground floor of the eighteenth-century refectory building, so as to make more room for cells. The Abbot kept a watchful eye on their work, bringing them up to the mark when necessary.

On leaving, I walked through the woods for a couple of hundred yards and turned round to look. Nestling inside its walls, the Lavra with its blue domes and crosses stood like something from another world. It seemed to float outside time and space. I have heard Russians say, "It is like Kitezh Gorod." The story is that the city of Kitezh was populous and happy. One day the Tartars advanced to destroy it, but before they arrived the whole city had disappeared beneath the waters of the lake, and if you go on the right day in summer — and people will still tell you where to go — you can hear the church bells of Kitezh.

CHAPTER V

The Baptists –
A Working-Class Movement

In Russia it is particularly difficult for foreigners to meet the working classes. One's natural contacts all tend to belong to the educated classes. Some of them started in peasant or worker families but as they have gone up in the world they have adopted a different style of life. The Russian Baptists are, however, a purely working-class movement, if for this purpose one may include the peasants in the working classes. Moreover, they are one of the few sections of the working classes which it is possible for a foreigner to get to know. The figures sometimes given about Baptist numbers are completely unreliable. All that can be said with certainty is that the movement has spread all over the Soviet Union. It seems to spread faster in large towns than in small towns.

Once a very irreligious Russian friend said to me, "When so many people have fallen away from religion, why is it that so many of the very best of the working class are becoming Baptists? I travel everywhere and now I find in Siberia that the most honest, hardest working and most intelligent workers are often converted by the Baptists."

It is fascinating to be among the real Russian working class. One hardly ever meets a Russian Baptist with a university education and nearly all of them have quite humble jobs. One reason for this is that anyone who is an openly practising Christian may find it hard to get a good job, or to get higher education for his children. So the Russian Baptists tend to be very simple people, but they are not therefore stupid. They represent that element in the working class which made the trade union movement in this country three or four generations ago.

The history of the Protestant and Protestantising elements in Russian spirituality is very interesting but it has been little studied. Western influence, which came not only through the German settlers in Russia but also through the British and Foreign Bible Society and occasional visitors such as Lord Radstock, is a part of the picture, but only a part. The Russian Orthodox Church threw up powerful spiritual forces which it was unable to contain, much as the Church of England threw up the Wesleys, but was unable to contain Methodism. For long the Protestantising tendencies in Russian religion were divided between a number of movements and denominations, but since 1945 most of them have been joined together in the Church of Evangelical Christians and Baptists in the U.S.S.R., which is commonly known as the Baptist Church.

In the past the relations between the Orthodox and the Baptists were those between a persecuting established Church and a persecuted non-conformity, but that has changed. Both Churches have now been through persecution together and have often found each other as Christian brothers. One still meets some of the old hostility among the rank and file on both sides, but the relations of the leaders are generally much better. I have even heard a very responsible member of the Orthodox Church say that the Baptists were raised up by God so that the Gospel might be heard in places where the Orthodox priests with their robes and other paraphernalia would not get a hearing. This particular person has always tried in his preaching to prepare the way for unity with the Baptists, but has to be very careful because "we Orthodox have such a bad record in this matter". He sees no objection to differences in forms of worship, and has more than once said to Baptist presbyters, "Why do you not let yourself be ordained as an Orthodox priest?" To which they always reply, "But what then is to become of those who hear us now?"

A Baptist service lasts two hours or a bit more and it has a definite beginning and a definite end, whereas an Orthodox service cross fades into the rest of life at both ends. So you can always find a Baptist church at any time within an hour of service by the stream of people walking towards it. They come early to meet their friends and they think nothing of coming to a long service three or four times a week. Go inside one of their churches and you see a crowd of good, ugly faces. It is like something from Hogarth, only transfigured. The service begins with a hymn, perhaps Moody and Sankey sung like a Russian folk song, perhaps a hymn from the Orthodox liturgy or perhaps something home grown. The Russian Baptists pour out new music every day; I am not sure how good most of it is but they sing it so well that it sounds good. Then a few verses of the Bible are read and the preacher expounds them in a sermon. After this one of the preachers leads in prayer and you notice a strange, subdued sound. There is none of the exhortation which sometimes spoils free prayer, no "Lord, as thou readest in the *Manchester Guardian* . . ." But the preacher puts a petition and each person turns it into his or her own words in a whisper. The whole church is filled with this scarcely audible whispering prayer and it binds everyone together. After this there are more hymns and the cycle starts again, scripture, sermon, prayer, hymns. And after that again, hymn, scripture, sermons prayer, hymn. Three sermons is the norm but there can be more. However, they are short and they are always worth hearing.

Once I was with the Moscow Baptists for the Breaking of Bread. They have Communion once a month and I have known Orthodox turn Baptist because the Baptist Church gives them Communion more often. At the service I attended large loaves were broken into pieces by the deacons and passed round on twelve very large patens to the two thousand five hundred people in church; then good strong alcoholic wine was passed round in twelve chalices. You stand for a moment as you make your communion and then pass the elements on to your neighbour and sit down.

We had a magnificent eucharistic sermon about the wounds of Christ. His wounds remind us of what he did and place us where the apostles stood. They strengthen us for the trials of life; and there was a good deal about trials and troubles which we were told to apply to our own experience; one could see that going home as one watched all those splendid ugly faces. Thomas doubted and we doubt, but the Lord comes and gives us his peace. Doubting Thomas was allowed to feel the Lord's wounds with his own hands. We too can feel the Lord's wounds in the bread and wine. This was the main theme and it was embroidered with much sound, traditional scriptural exposition; the Exodus from Egypt was a "type" of the passion, manna was a "type" of the bread from heaven and so on. It would have been accepted as thoroughly sound eucharistic doctrine in Westminster Cathedral, Westminster Abbey or the Bloomsbury Central Baptist Church. I doubt greatly whether the preacher had read any of the Fathers of the Church but it was their doctrine he was giving us. In ways such as this the Russian Baptists are much nearer to the Orthodox than you could have guessed. They do not formally accept the Nicene Creed but I should be surprised to find they dispute any of its teachings.

Another time I was at the baptism of forty-three men and women. A largish pool at the foot of the pulpit was filled with water and the Presbyter stood in water above his waist while the candidates, robed in white as their name indicates, descended one by one, men from one side and women from the other, to be baptised by total immersion in the name of the Trinity. As each man came forward he made his profession of faith in his own words. I had an angel's eye view from a raised tribune, and it was indeed a sight for angels to see their transformed faces as they rose wet and glistening from the waters of baptism.

Each congregation seems the same but each is different. There are large bodies of Baptists among the Russians in Central Asia and I once spent eight days visiting their congregations with the Rev. John Pollock and his wife Anne. The congregation at Tashkent were real Russian working-class people and many of them must have begun life as peasants. We met in a church on the outskirts of Tashkent on a weekday evening, when it was

raining cats and dogs so that the side-streets became very muddy
indeed, and the city transport was disorganised by the arrival
of Fidel Castro. Even so, about three hundred people came.
The church had been burnt a year before and had not been
rebuilt (and still has not been rebuilt). So they sat in a tent with
the unburnt part of the church serving as a chancel. On my
right were bearded Tolstoyan figures, such as I never expected
to see in real life; the women, who all wore head scarves, sat in
front of me and I could see their faces best. One could see what
went home to each of them, who knew temptation, who had
doubts, who had suffered, but all of them showed love, joy and
peace. They were very simple people but strong in their
simplicity and more intelligent, I should think, than most
educated congregations. There were a good many skilled
workers among them but no white-collared workers, so far as I
could see, above the social rank of a bank clerk. One clever-
looking man turned out to be a retired sea captain; he could
hardly have got further from the sea than Tashkent. They were
of all ages, both men and women. A striking youngish man with
a black beard was the deacon; his chief job is to visit the sick
to give them communion and to bury the dead.

The reading was from Revelation vii: "After this I beheld,
and lo, a great multitude which no man could number, of all
nations and kindreds and people and tongues, stood before the
throne and before the Lamb . . ." This showed us the end of the
Christian life when faith and hope would have achieved their
aim and only love would remain to all eternity. This final
reunion of all blessed souls was prefigured by the meetings on
earth of those who loved each other in the Lord. This evening
three people had come from another land, there were only three
and yet tears of joy could be seen. What then would be the joy
of that meeting in heaven? We all cried and after two hours of
hymns and prayers and Bible reading John Pollock gave a short
message on the text Hebrews xiii, 8: "Jesus Christ the same
yesterday, and today and for ever". I then spoke in Russian on
Acts xvii, 26–8: "He hath made of one blood all nations for to
dwell on the face of the earth . . ." They always listen to every

word and I found that five years later my words were remembered. Then after a hymn we kissed the Presbyter and sat down to strawberries and cream cakes with the leading members of the congregation, or rather with the men; the women stood around and served us and were introduced to us, but did not sit down. This meal was called a *trapeza*, a word that I only knew as meaning a meal with monks or nuns in a refectory.

This was the first of a number of pleasant Central Asian evenings, seated round the table with our Baptist brothers, when they made us tell our life stories and they told us theirs. Once after strawberries and cakes, cherries, pomegranates and biscuits, all displayed on pretty china, I was told to say a few words. So I told my story as a typical story for the intelligentsia of my generation; in the West the educated had been the first to turn against religion and would be the first to turn again to Christianity. This was thought interesting, but they said that in Russia religion is going from simple people into the intelligentsia. Then it was their turn to tell their stories. The Presbyter, an elderly peasant with bushy moustaches, said that he had been brought up in a religious family as an Orthodox but that he had paid no particular attention to religion till 1934, long after he was grown up. Then suddenly he felt a strong desire to save his soul; and he knew the way to do that was to take up his cross. So he made himself an enormous wooden cross, which he proposed to carry on his shoulder for a hundred kilometres. He got the priest to bless the cross, but then the most awful weather began with rain first and afterwards knee-deep snow, so that he could not start for a week and people began to laugh at him. Then an old Baptist woman came and told him that that wasn't the sort of cross he had to take up. He believed her and had more talks with her. At first his wife, who sat smiling as he told the story, was angry with him for making himself a laughing-stock by making the cross and then not carrying it, but in the end they both became Baptists. After that they did not know what to do with the cross, but some drunks came and took it away.

Another Presbyter was a rather more educated man. Brought

up in a believing family, he took no interest in religion till the war. Then he saw many people die and he watched their last moments attentively. This made him think about life and death, and he began to be aware that God was watching over him and that his life was being preserved for a purpose. He began to pray in moments of difficulty, and in one moment of great danger he promised that he would give his life to God if He got him out of his jeopardy. But he soon forgot his promise. When eventually he was baptised it was in an icy river in January, but he felt quite warm. The brethren asked him to speak to them but he was afraid. So they prayed for him for a week. After that he had to speak, and so he became a preacher. Someone said this illustrated the way in which the Baptists find good Presbyters without any theological college to train them at. They have about thirty thousand preachers, which means thirty thousand missionaries, or so they said. (This figure is quite possible but I do not think anyone knows how many Russian Baptist preachers there are.) When the late Metropolitan Nicholas was told this, he said, "You have far more than thirty thousand. Among you every old woman is a missionary."

From Tashkent we flew to Dushanbe (formerly Stalinabad), the capital of Tadjikistan, and flying above the clouds we could see the snowy peaks of the Pamirs, the "roof of the world". Here one is, and one feels, nearer to the Khyber Pass than to Moscow. The Tadjik women, who are very beautiful, wear a cross between the Punjabi Moslem dress and the Uzbek; they wear pyjama-like trousers of Uzbek silk with silk robes on top and an embroidered Tartar skull cap. The men wear Russian boots, striped silk robes and skull caps.

These towns of Russian Turkestan are rather like British India. There is a European quarter with broad streets and a native quarter with narrow lanes. In Dushanbe Russians and Tadjiks were living together in rickety one-storey houses, but the people looked clean, and the Tadjik women did not have that oppressed look one sees in some Moslem countries. The schoolgirls were ragging about like anywhere else. I tried to find the Mosque but I reckoned that the Russians would not know where it was and that if I spoke to a Tadjik woman it might be misunderstood. The atmosphere in all the towns is very Moslem, and it is surprisingly hard to find natives who speak Russian well enough for a proper conversation. It is much easier to find English speakers in the corresponding Indian towns. Eventually I found a Tadjik boy who spoke Russian; he was carrying a bucket. "What? What? Oh our Mosque." And he told me the way. Soon I saw a picturesque old man leaning on a stick and I felt sure I was near the Mosque. In fact he was leaning against its door. I went in and found a delectable court-yard with poplar trees and a veranda-like Mosque with great carved wooden pillars in the eighteenth-century Persian style. I found that it had been greatly enlarged in the last three or four years, and I don't think any of it can be more than forty years old, but evidently the traditional style was alive.

It was a Friday and time for prayers. About a thousand men were assembled and prayed devoutly, though my presence was a distraction. Afterwards I made friends with some bearded men whom I understand to be Imams and Qazis. They invited me to tea with their entourage and we parted affectionately. None of them knew enough Russian for a serious conversation, but they said they had most friendly relations with the Christians and they were anxious to understand what it is that we really believe. Two of the Imams had studied for twenty years at the Koranic school in Bokhara "in the peaceful time", which I took to mean before the Revolution. In some out of the way place in Kazakhstan, I was told by the Baptists, a group of Moslems had come to their *mullah* saying, "It is a long way to the Mosque but there is a Baptist church near us. Can we go to it?" "Yes, certainly," was the reply. "They believe in one God and they do not worship idols like the Orthodox." It was too early at that stage to say how the experiment was turning out.

On the way back from the Mosque I found a palatial *chai khaneh* with tall pillars and tables under the trees and couches with carpets on them. The Tadjiks sat on the couches and the Russians sat at the tables. I saw one Tadjik family but the rest of the men had left their wives at home. I drank an enormous

jorum of green tea out of a bowl and watched a man making
endless *shashlyk* over a large charcoal grill which had been made
ingeniously out of what looked like half a drainpipe.

The Baptist congregation at Dushanbe comes from eleven
different nationalities and half its members are Germans, who
were exiled to Central Asia in the war and have not been
allowed to return to their original homes in the Ukraine and on
the Volga. The German faces stood out in the congregation and
there were German as well as Russian texts on the walls. The
church is just a large oblong box but well built and beautifully
kept. Everything was well arranged with German thorough-
ness and there was a penthouse to hang one's hat and coat in.
The German element in the congregation makes it different,
more staid and socially superior, but the mixture of races *gees*.
The service was half in Russian and half in German. A slit-eyed,
swarthy Kazakh, one of the few converts from Islam, was sitting
in the front row and joined heartily in the German hymns; one
of these was about the Second Coming and, both in words and
music, it seemed to be a sacred analogue of "She'll be coming
round the mountain". The service was like that at Tashkent,
except that in this more German atmosphere it ended with
hand-shakes instead of kisses.

Afterwards we went to the house of one of the brethren, a
dear little bungalow with a shady courtyard; simple but
spacious and clean. We were told more life stories. A youngish
woman said she had grown up without religion. She thought
icons were just pieces of wood and that no harm would come to
you if you scratched their eyes out. For this her friends called
her an antichrist. After that her husband was murdered. Then
one day through a wall she heard some Baptists singing. Soon
after that she made friends with a Baptist family, who began to
take her to church, and she and all her children were converted.

From Dushanbe we flew to Samarkand in Uzbekistan over
small green valleys, and vast expanses of mountain that looked
very bare even after the rain. One can see why Tadjikistan
played so little part in history. Samarkand on the other hand lies
in well-watered land, and is all that one expects it to be, even

including "such sweet jams meticulously jarred, as God's own prophet eats in paradise". What I have to say about the architectural splendours of Samarkand has already been said in my book *Life in Russia*, which was written after a previous visit in 1944. Many writers have described Samarkand but not many have noticed the Baptist church there. It is a well-built little building with its own garden, like most of the houses in Samarkand. The Baptist community here had been established thirty years before, but still had less than two hundred baptised members. They were rather apologetic about their slow growth and explained that Samarkand is a bit of a backwater. The Church grows more quickly in the larger industrial towns, which is not what one has been taught to expect. The local community had turned out in force and the little church was full. There was less variety among the congregation but everything else was there, including a largish choir, who attempted some difficult pieces, not with complete success.

After the service we had supper in the house of an agronomist. It had no plumbing but apart from that it was a pretty good house with several fair-sized rooms and a garden of eight hundred square metres which the proprietor put to good use, being an agronomist. The houses here are bungalows, generally well-built and always with gardens in which vines and fruit trees give shade in the heat as well as fruit. Good pensions are now paid in the Soviet Union and when people retire, many of them like to move from Siberia to the warmer climate of Turkestan. So, Samarkand could easily become the Soviet Cheltenham.

I learnt in conversation over supper that the Baptists have a strong prejudice against their Presbyters being unmarried. Indeed they refuse to ordain a man unless he is married and, if his wife dies, they make him marry again, unless he is very old indeed. This is one of those cases where the Russian Baptists have been unconsciously influenced by the Orthodox, who also ordain only married men, unless indeed they are monks. But if an Orthodox priest's wife dies, he can never marry again. All this came out because the Senior Presbyter asked about British

missionaries. "I suppose they are all Baptists?" "Oh no. All
the Churches send missionaries overseas. The Church of England has more than two thousand." "Tell me about them. I
will pray for them. Are any of them unmarried?" "Yes, quite a
number." "But that must lead to trouble." "Very seldom."
Great surprise.

Alma Ata, the last stop in our tour of Central Asia, is an old
Tsarist garrison town successfully converted into a modern
city. Lying on a lush green plateau two thousand feet above
sea-level, surrounded by famous apple orchards, and with
mountains and lakes within easy reach, it is one of the nicest
places in the Soviet Union. There are two flourishing Baptist
churches there with a combined membership of about two
thousand. They must nearly all have been present at the special
combined service that we attended in one of the churches. The
predominant element was bright-eyed boys and girls in their
late 'teens or early twenties. They looked unusually sophisticated for Russian working-class people, some of the girls were
without head-scarves and their clothes were distinctly *with it*. I
was to speak by request about the work for peace of the British
Churches and I found that there was a better case to be made
than I had expected. What I had to say was completely strange
to them but I watched their eager faces carefully and they took
it all in, when I told them of discussions with ministers and
generals. These Russian Baptist congregations can understand
anything. I have had a good deal of experience of speaking to
them and have never had the feeling that anything was going
over their heads. But you must put things in the way that they
understand. If you are speaking in church, you must not joke,
you must start from Scripture and you must show how what
you are saying flows from Scripture. Some of their Presbyters
have studied recently at Spurgeon's College and at the Baptist
Theological College in Bristol. It can be interesting to hear them
expounding up-to-date western ideas to their Muscovite hearers.
After the service the congregation were told to depart in peace
and go back to their own homes. I wondered what it was that we
were not supposed to discover from them, but I asked no

questions. Before we left the church all the women shook me by the hand and all the men kissed me on the lips, and such wet kisses.

Supper was a very leisurely meal at the house of one of the congregation. An old man of eighty told us his story. He came of a devout Orthodox family but did not pay much attention to religion. About 1907 he was a sailor in the navy and religion got him. He became determined to have a vision. He prayed and prayed in one of the St. Petersburg churches and once he thought he saw something, but it vanished. He tried with his eyes open and his eyes shut, but nothing happened. Then after many months he found a Bible in the house of a Baptist and began to read it, but he did not dare bring it into the naval barracks. Then he began to have doubts and these centred on one problem: "Who was Cain's wife?" There was no-one to ask. There was a priest in the barracks but he was "worse than the boss". At last he was discharged from the navy and went back to his home in Siberia. One day he was travelling with a very old priest and he plucked up his courage and asked him, "Who was Cain's wife?" "He took a wife from China." But he said, that wouldn't do. So the priest gave a new answer: "It was after the Flood." When that was rejected, he said, "It was when they were building the Tower of Babel." "I saw that if I pressed the question far enough, he would answer, 'Cain married my daughter.' And he was almost old enough." This shook his confidence in the Orthodox Church. So he got a Bible and began to read it more and more. At first the village priest praised him for this but when he refused to venerate icons, he called him an antichrist and told the villagers they could only save their souls if they killed him. A crowd of about a thousand collected and there was a lot of shouting and confusion. He just managed to make them hear, and said, "If I have injured any-one, let him strike me, but if not, let me go." In the end no-one touched him. His wife was very angry with him for getting into such a scrape, but she thought she had better read the Bible, too. "She read day and night, seeking the truth," and in the end she agreed with her husband. They were both baptised and from that time he became an evangelist. All this was told with humour and fire, and with so many old-fashioned Russian phrases that one was carried back to another age. But here was the old man, as straight as a ramrod, still looking like the A.B. that he once was, wearing a white yachting cap in Central Asia and converting the souls of particularly intelligent Russian workmen and their wives in the nineteen-sixties.

CHAPTER VI

Pskov

In August and September 1968 I spent six weeks wandering round Russia looking up old friends, making new friends, spending astronomical hours in church to my very great profit, and enjoying the hundred and one incidents that make up a day. I hoped to revisit Novgorod after thirty-four years, but before that I decided to visit the ancient city of Pskov. So I booked myself to spend a week there. I had taken a seat on a day-train from Leningrad, but the rule was that foreigners must travel by night. What was I supposed not to see? In Pskov they did not seem to know the rule and I returned by day, looking out of the window at the very green countryside with endless birch and pine broken by little clearings in the forest, which became more frequent as we approached Leningrad. The hay was still in stooks on the 16th August which reminded me how far north we were. There were a good many potato patches in the waste land beside the railway, and each of them must have been the joy of some countryman's heart. It was a quietly smiling landscape which reminded me of Maurice Baring's remark that after you have known Russia for a few years you suddenly become aware that that flat and apparently dull landscape has become infinitely dear to you.

On the way out I travelled hard class, which was no hardship, being rather more comfortable than a couchette in western Europe. There were four of us in the compartment, a priggish British civil servant, who tended to hog the conversation, a blue-stocking teacher of English, and a pretty, well-dressed medical student with fluffy hair on her way to stay with Polish friends in Cracow; she was seen off by a charming sophisticated couple who would have looked at home in Paris or London; such people are still a small minority but they are the trend setters. The blue-stocking ticked me off for saying "Russia" instead of "the Soviet Union". I said I meant Russia and soon fell into a deep sleep. The conductress woke me firmly at four and made sure I had not nicked any of the bed linen. I got out sleepily in the dark and was greeted in Russian by a friendly girl from Intourist. "But how did you know I speak Russian?" "We discussed that, and decided that no-one would come to Pskov by himself for a week unless he spoke Russian."

I felt at once that Pskov is slower and more easy-going, more like Ireland, more like what Russia would be if the Russians were left alone. Here is an older, quieter Russia, where people live their own lives.

I was given a comfortable room at the hotel and had some more sleep. When I woke up the hotel restaurant was shut, and so was the buffet, but I wheedled my way into the buffet and had an excellent cold snack. The waitress sat down with her clientele—I wasn't the only person who had got in while the buffet was shut—and I soon got drawn into the conversation. Two young actors belonging to a theatre company from Velikiye Luki, who were touring the collective farms in this area, were discussing with the waitress the problem of getting fat and what the first signs were when your tummy begins to stick out.

We sat gossiping for the best part of an hour, during which I got some good tips about the local sights. Until the beginning of the sixteenth century Pskov was an independent city-republic with its own traditions, which have never quite died out. Pskov had its own style of architecture, very simple and very original; the elements are always the same, domes, apses, belfries, porches and side chapels, but they are combined in a different way for every church; there must be some underlying scheme of proportions, but I could not guess what it was. From the fifteenth century the Pskov architects made use of asymmetry in a way that I thought was unknown outside China till the eighteenth century. Every church is unmistakably Pskovsky, and unmistakably original. The problems of modern architecture are similar, and modern architects could learn from Pskov something about how to use simple elements in an individual way.

I strolled out slowly and began to admire the many historic churches from the outside. Some were open for worship, but even they were closed for the afternoon till five-thirty when they opened for Saturday vespers; in the Orthodox Church every celebration of the Liturgy (Holy Communion) in the morning is prepared for by an evening service on the previous day. Many churches were closed altogether or used as warehouses, but all were carefully whitewashed and looked very pretty. The Cathedral of the Trinity is the principal church and it is open. I was told that Pushkin, whose home was not far away, had this church and its square in mind when he was writing *Boris Godunov*. The cathedral stands in the Pskov Kremlin on a point jutting out between the peat-brown waters of the Pskov river, which is little more than a brook, and the clear blue waters of the broad Velikaya. I had a recommendation to the Bishop and I asked an old woman carrying two buckets on a yoke where his house was. She led me to another elderly woman, also drawing water from an outdoor tap—and this in a place that was the equivalent of the close of Salisbury Cathedral; but it is only fair to add that all the houses were scheduled for demolition. "That is the deacon's wife. What a wonderful voice he has! But he is away on holiday." Then, turning to the deacon's wife, "I haven't seen you for a long time." "If you have not seen me, it's because you didn't want to see me"—the Russians can be outspoken in personal relations. Blushes ensued with a confused explanation and the conversation went on. They told me which bus to take to the Bishop's house on the outskirts of the town. I soon found it, a well-built, rather distinguished two-storey house standing among old-fashioned Russian one-storey houses, each with its plot of land. The people here looked contented and would, I thought, have every reason to be so, if they all had piped water. I was hailed by an elderly Pole who was working in his garden and took me for a friend of his called Samoilov. My Russian accent has deteriorated with time and I am sometimes told that I have a

Jewish accent, but some of my friends deny this. In Pskov I was generally taken for a Soviet citizen from nearby Esthonia, a country that has kept many of its western traditions. But on occasions I have been taken for a Russian émigré, of whom many now visit the country of their birth, for a Frenchman, or for anything but what I am.

I knocked at the Bishop's gate and it was cautiously opened by a funny little bearded old man who looked at me suspiciously and then kissed me affectionately three times, put me to sit on a bench and asked whether I played chess. A woman darted out of a little hut and had a mysterious fierce argument with him about a salad. "My eyes hurt me and even so they give me no peace." I soon concluded that he was more than a little mad. However, he called a pale young priest with a sharp nose and for a moment I had hopes that they were going to put me on a bus and send me to stay the night at the monastery described in an earlier chapter, but they decided, rightly, that they had no authority to do that. And the Bishop was away conducting a Bulgarian church delegation round his diocese.

I strolled back to the centre and had a snack at a *pelmennaya* that I had had my eye on since the morning. A *pelmennaya* is the equivalent of a *pizzeria* in Italy or a fried fish shop in England. You get cheap food in the national style, and it can be good. *Pelmeny* are small Siberian dumplings. Both food and service were excellent; the *pelmeny* and some soup I had first had been cooked slowly and lovingly; the waitress wiped the table before serving me; and there was no queue.

Compare this with my experience in Leningrad two days earlier, when I had lunch in a snack bar on the Nevsky Prospekt. It took an hour, of which ten minutes were spent eating. First you queue to pay, then you queue to get what you have ordered, and then you eat, standing at a breast-high table. It was not bad when you got it, but the customers obviously disliked the uncivilised service. Three fat women were doing their best to dish things out but everything was badly organised, so that the staff kept getting in each other's way. It must have been very trying for them and one of them became very angry and started shouting at the public; no-one could understand her grievance; I think she was just blowing off steam; at any rate she quieted down as suddenly as she had blown up, and after that all was smiles. No attempt was made to dry or even drain the plates. Your helping was often sloshed into a pool of water, but I was lucky and got a fairly dry plate. On another occasion at a slack time of day I ate at this snack bar without waiting in a queue; the plates were dry and I could hardly believe that the quiet friendly girls who served us were the furies whom I had met on my first visit; but they were, and I saw portraits of women who must have been their ancestresses among the eighteenth-century pictures in the Russky Muzey.

For evensong Pskov's cathedral was full. It took half an hour for the people to queue to have their foreheads anointed; the priest does it with what might be a child's paint brush, and I wondered what happens when a girl with a fringe comes along, as some did. At one point there was a procession of candles on long wands decorated with wild flowers. The great majority of the congregation were women of all ages from seventeen to eighty. I saw three children. A sad old woman told me it was better to die than to live. She was not married and came of that generation whose lives were spoiled by the war, and by what went before and after it. She was applying for an old age pension, which one can get comparatively young—their hard life ages the Russians quickly—but being an unskilled worker she did not expect to get much. She lived in a miserable tumbledown building and could get nothing better, but "there is plenty of room in the cemeteries."

As I went out I was stopped by four seventeen-year-old girls who had heard who I was. They were all awaiting the result of their examination to see if they would get into the Teachers' Training College here. They lived in a hostel and had to feed themselves on twenty-eight roubles* a month. They said the hostel was bearable, but no-one is keen on these hostels. What

* The exchange value of a rouble is about a dollar but according to some careful American calculations its purchasing value is only about half its exchange value. Any such comparisons are however very approximate, for the Soviet price system is different from that of a free economy. A hundred kopeks make up a rouble.

would our students do if they were told to manage on less than ten shillings or a dollar a day? They asked eagerly first about other countries and then about myself. "Are you married?" "Yes." "Have you any children?" "No." "That is very strange. Why not?"

I had an excellent supper at the hotel, served without any delay, but I was put in a corner by myself and anyone who came and talked to me was shooed away. On my table was a flag labelled U.S.S.R. in big letters and Intourist in small letters, which was supposed to show that I was untouchable; but in fact it made one man come up to me thinking that I must represent a Soviet football team. He was soon chased away, but I went and sat with him afterwards and asked whether I looked like a *futbolist*. Every evening I went through the same farce several times. Someone would come and ask politely whether I minded his sitting at my table. "Of course not." And in a few minutes the staff would come and chase him off. But this did not prevent us exchanging winks. One day I sat with a very intelligent group of well-dressed men who were obviously too important for the management to shoo them away. They ignored me completely but I could see that they were journalists; so I listened for a bit and then electrified them by joining in the conversation and saying who I was. They were the staff of one of the literary magazines, and not one of the more progressive of these. One of them had a complete file of the *Britansky Soyuznik*, which he frequently consulted. "Your idea was absolutely right but there were conservatives here who did not understand what you were trying to do."

At the weekend all the *with it* youth of Pskov were in the restaurant enjoying the evening with a good dinner and quite a good band to dance to. Many of them danced solo in the modern way with a good deal of style. I doubt if the food would have been quite as good at Fortt's restaurant in Bath, which is a fair comparison, but the people would have been a little better dressed. Bath, however, has many other restaurants, five of them in the *Good Food Guide*, whereas Pskov has only three full blown restaurants, this, one at the station and one across the river. Every medium-sized town in Europe has a restaurant of this kind, but I doubt whether the type exists in North America unless perhaps in a place like Quebec.

I think the nearness of the Baltic Republics "the Soviet abroad", makes Pskov a bit more sophisticated, but on week-days the crowd was much less smart. They danced sedately in couples, as one did many years ago and there was none of the fireworks that I saw at the weekend.

One evening I got into conversation with an elderly man, with a sad, long face. When the Germans took Pskov, they put him in prison and eventually carried him off to Munich, but he escaped and finally ended up in South America more or less by accident. For twenty years he made a living there as a bad but dogged photographer. Eventually, having had no news of his family, he decided to come home. Back in Russia he inquired again through the Russian Red Cross who found that his wife, his son, his daughter and the grandchildren he has never seen were all living in the country from which he had just come.

One afternoon I went round to see him and found him living in a slit of a room with a large iron stove which was heated even in summer. He had two South American parrots in a cage, a tree in a pot, which was supposed to be a lemon tree, lots of little bottles, some odds and ends of food, a bed, an upright chair, some suitcases and not much else. His supply of food was in enamel containers on a small table. He had a good pension from the state and was not short of money. Three people came to see him while I was there and I did not think he was lonely except in the sense that the only people he wants to see are his family whom he has not seen for twenty-five years. He showed me their photographs and says the Soviet government are quite ready to facilitate his journey; but the South American country, where his family are, refuses on principle to give a visa to any Soviet citizen or even to accept an affidavit from the Soviet Union. I suggested there might be a way round through my Church contacts, he gave me various addresses and as I write the matter is being investigated, not without hope.

There was not a service in the Cathedral every day but, when there was one, I went. On Sunday there were more men than on Saturday evening but the congregation was not quite so large. They were mainly, but not entirely, working-class people. The elder women had their arms well covered and wore scarves with much better colours than a few years before. The younger women wore sleeveless dresses and had bare heads. There were six or seven nuns. A few people seem to have come in out of curiosity and looked lost, but most were praying fervently. After the service the Dean asked whether I was not John Lawrence and reminded me that I had visited him in Jerusalem when he had been head of the Moscow Patriarchate's monastery there.

As the days went by, the Cathedral grew on me, with its silver domes rising above the Kremlin and towering over the two rivers. The conception is very simple. Inside four plain, square, white pillars shoot up to an enormous height, carrying one with them. The eighteenth-century gilt iconostasis (altar screen) is one of the highest I have ever seen, but the rest of the decoration is quite low. When it got dark the rococo gilt church furniture glittered with candles and electric light. At all times it was made very pretty with flowers; and at nearly all times there was a corpse in a coffin with its face showing standing near the entrance.

I took a liking to the hotel, which was friendly and efficient in essentials, but there were lapses. Fresh flowers in my room but no hot water. One day they never made my bed and left my breakfast uncleared away. When I pointed this out to one of the maids, she said, "Akh! They didn't do the little bit of cleaning." And no further action was taken. In the restaurant they never kept me waiting, but also they never gave me a plate for the main course. So I ate it out of the dish, like a dog, but it tasted the same. One cleans one's own shoes and there was a place to do it at the foot of the stairs with a brush and shoe polish. But there was only one brush for all colours, and it was so worn away, and the shoe polish was so dried up that it was almost useless.

In my long wanderings in the streets everyone over thirty seemed to have a desperately determined look. Sometimes I

6

think that the Soviet people have suffered too much for too long, and then one sees one of those faces, more often in a woman but sometimes in men, which have a tranquillity that, it seems, nothing could shake. Many of these are Christians, but not all of them. The young have suffered less and are more easy-going. In Leningrad couples went hand in hand and even with arms round waists. In Pskov the older puritanical conventions were still maintained but I would not give this strictness much longer and in Pskov's agreeable parks it was already breaking down. Most of the films showing had slushy sexy titles, like western films and most unlike the Soviet Union a few years earlier. One film showing was the Czech *Closely Observed Trains*. No doubt it was taken off quickly after the invasion of Czecho-slovakia, which lay a few days ahead. And I am bound to say that this sort of naughty film would have made short work of Stalinist conventions—I will not say Stalinist morals, for it was all eyewash. What went on when nobody was looking was nobody's business.

Women's hair was more cared for than five years earlier. I saw beehives, horse's tails, fringes and buns but most of the coiffures were nondescript fluffy. Much dye was used, often unsuccessfully, but some of the girls looked stunning. For men a medium-short, old-fashioned cut seemed universal, and there were many fewer shaven or closely cropped heads than a few years earlier. There were some fine beards and moustaches but no fancy whiskers or sideburns. In Leningrad there were girls with long hair flowing loose, but not in Pskov.

Window shopping was interesting. The provincial towns used to be starved of consumer goods so that to their inhabitants Moscow seemed a paradise. Now the difference was closing fast. In Pskov you could get modern furniture at a reasonable price and clothes that were up to the average Moscow standard. And there were specialist shops. A sports shop with goods run-ning from motor bicycles to fishing rods and camping equip-ment. A shop for artists' paints and brushes. A chemist's shop with a fine display of herbal remedies, including a special sec-tion for plants from the Pskov region; the Russians love herbal

remedies and are, incidentally, surprisingly easily taken in by
quack doctoring. In the kiosks there were greetings cards for
various occasions, a thing I had not seen before; they all took
the occasion straight; there was no guying. And there was a
special little shop for glass jars, the Russians being great
picklers. I saw one woman carrying with great care a little jar
full of wild-strawberry jam.

In Pskov, for all the determined look of the older citizens, I
hardly saw the harassed faces and the suspicious gait, which
one takes for granted in Moscow. People were strolling in the
streets, or in the parks of which they are justly proud, thinking
of how they will gather mushrooms, what jars they will buy for
marinading "white mushrooms", what flowers they will grow
on their little plot somewhere in the country and where they
will fish and shoot. It is not for nothing that the Soviet Union
suddenly broke into the international market for sporting guns,
though it may be a long time before Soviet fishing rods can
compete in the west; these, however, are sold in very large
numbers for local use.

Water plays a great part in the amenities of Pskov. Boys bathe
in the shallow waters of the Pskov river and play about in boats
beside women doing their laundry in the river, and a hydrofoil
will take one down the Velikaya through Lake Peipus to Narva
on the Gulf of Finland. A ferry supplements the too few bridges
to take one across the Velikaya, which is a little broader than
the Thames at Windsor. A bridge is being rebuilt completely so
as not to spoil a view of the Kremlin, and no high buildings are
allowed. Pskov was of an enormous size for a mediaeval city
and the walls are being carefully restored to their original
appearance.

I had discovered by chance that there was a Baptist church in
Pskov and I found one could get to it by a pleasant walk over a
footbridge across the Pskov river. It was originally the chapel of
the German cemetery, a plain little neo-Gothic building which
had a certain cosy charm and was decorated with florid texts in
Russian, mostly from St. John. The community has existed for
eighty years but has remained small. On a weekday evening the

little chapel was full but not crowded with a congregation of about forty, of whom one in five were men. The service was as usual, except that they knelt for prayer and that the prayer came not from the Presbyter, but from the body of the congregation, as in evangelical prayer meetings in England. Various women prayed aloud in turn while the congregation whispered their petitions under their breath in their own words and there were cries of "Amen", as well as groans and quite a loud sound of snuffling. First they gave thanks, and prayed "not only for our church but for all churches". Then they prayed for their children with torrential prayers, such as Monica must have prayed for the young Augustine. Handkerchiefs were out, many tears were shed, and it seemed irresistible.

I sat at the back but, when they heard who I was, I was asked "to expound the word of God". So I spoke with such simple words as came to me about love and unity, using John xvii as a text. Afterwards I walked back with the congregation. They reminded me of the faithful, slow-spoken west country people among whom I was brought up. The people of Pskov are called *Skobars* or scrapers, as the Tynesiders are called Geordies, and these spoke with the broad, slovenly accent of the true *Skobar*, which is hard to follow, but they were very lively and amusing. "Do the English men drink vodka? My word! How the Russians drink! Oy oy oy!" "Do you have icons in the Church of England?" "No, but stained-glass windows." "Yes, I know. I've seen them in Riga." And they wanted to know exactly what subjects are portrayed in stained-glass windows. "Do you have the Transfiguration? Next Monday is the Transfiguration and we are having a special service."

My last day was spent seeing the more splendid and more inaccessible sights, for which I had to hire a car. This is the great flax-growing district and is called Blue Russia, from the tiny blue flax flowers which are supposed to be the same colour as the *Skobar* eyes. I was shown how after the flax is cut it is cunningly done up into little twists so that the rain runs off it. How the *Skobars* love their city and its countryside! And every turn of the road had its story. Very intelligent Russians were seeing the same sights as me and we had some interesting conversation. One needs a special permit to see the fourteenth-century frescoes of the Snetogorsk Monastery, which are only now being uncovered but will become world famous when their cleaning is finished. A group of top experts were to be settled in the monastery grounds later in the year to concentrate on the job. The frescoes are very free and original. There is a painting of Pentecost which gets right away from the fixed traditional composition of Byzantine art. One of the saints has his hair standing straight on end in a most un-Byzantine way. And the angel of the Annunciation has a beautiful strict face, rather frightening. We looked at it for a long time and then one of the Russians said, "I expect Gabriel is really like that."

Next morning I got up at five-thirty and went regretfully to the station to catch the early train to Leningrad. "Look," said the guide who had met me earlier a week before, "the summer is over"; and she pointed sadly to a little wedge of cranes already beginning their migration; but that day was the hottest of the summer and yet hotter days were to come.

CHAPTER VII

Again in Novgorod

Back in Leningrad my chief concern was to get to Novgorod, which proved almost as difficult as it had been thirty-four years earlier. I tried to book myself to Novgorod from London but Intourist said it could not be done. This was nonsense but it seemed better to wait and sort it out in Leningrad. Here they said that of course it was possible, but I must pay more than fourteen pounds for changing my mind. "But I haven't changed my mind. It is simply that your people in London mis-led me." They then got instructions from higher up and even sent a telegram to Moscow, who made all sorts of difficulties and still insisted on their fourteen pounds, in spite of the clear meaning of their regulations, which they showed me. I became very angry and told them that this was robbery and a *bezobrazie*, which is a *Frechheit* in German and can't be translated into English, and they had better get that over to their bosses or there would be trouble. The chief boss seemed to be taking cover and was never available on the telephone, but the next morning I went round and caught him at his office. I explained in my mildest manner that there had been a misunderstanding — anything else was unthinkable. He said he knew all about my case and put me in charge of a nice lady with green eyes who arranged everything in a trice.

What was it all about? I do not know, but I can make a good guess. The Intourist office in London were lazy and thought it would save them trouble if they told me I could not stay the night in Novgorod. Then in Leningrad Intourist kept trying to squeeze extra payments out of me on various pretexts. To an old Moscow hand the reason for this was obvious; it had been planned that they were to earn an impossible amount of foreign exchange and they were determined to get their money by hook or crook. If they failed, they would be in trouble. In the Soviet Union the goals of the plan laid down for every enterprise are rigid, but the means by which it is obtained can be flexible. By arguing I once got the price of a ticket from Leningrad to Helsinki reduced by a half with the help of some useful advice from a friendly Intourist girl.

My sister-in-law, who, by coincidence, was in Leningrad at the same time, had a similar experience. She had paid for an hotel room but Intourist had calmly put her and her party in tents on a camping site where the beds were sopping wet. Highly centralised planning on the Soviet model is apt to have disagreeable side effects. An edict goes forth that production is to go up and that more foreign exchange is to be earned. No-one is effectively consulted about the probable effects and it often happens that the only way of carrying out the plan is to find some way of doing someone else down, by cheating the customers, exploiting the workers, or any one of a thousand and one dodges known to Soviet managers. The capitalist system creates waste by unemployment and by leaving resources unused or only partly used. The Communist system creates waste by its rigidity, which puts obstacles in the way of productive change and causes very wasteful friction because people feel they are being mucked about.

In speaking of these particular troubles to the Soviet authorities afterwards, I did not make them a cause of complaint; but I did suggest that the attempt to earn foreign exchange in these ways was bad for public relations.

In Leningrad I told people how much I had liked the quieter rhythm of Pskov and they looked pleased. Leningrad, they said, was less hectic than Moscow and that was one reason why they preferred it.

I made some enjoyable acquaintances with some working-class people who I had the good luck to see several times each. One, a man in his forties, had been a sailor in the war and had fought through the siege of Leningrad. "My father and four of my brothers died in the siege and my other brother was killed in

the war. I alone am left. My mother is alive, but how can one
live after what she has been through?" He was the sort of man
that Sir Bernard Pares and Maurice Baring must always have
been meeting at the beginning of the century. The salt of the
thoughtful working class, and a deeply Christian man. "There
are eighteen churches and houses of prayer open in Leningrad,
fourteen Orthodox churches, one Catholic church, one Baptist
prayer house, one mosque and one synagogue. And there is the
Old Believers' church over there, but it is closed. There is a wonderful book about the Old Believers, *In the Forests* by Melnikov-
Pechersky." This is one of the untranslated Russian classics, not,
I am pretty sure, reprinted in Soviet days, certainly not easy to
come by, and requiring rather a special culture to read, for it
abounds in strange words used only in the Old Believers' community. Where else would you find working-class people who
read this sort of book and yet stay working class? "Yes," I said,
"it is a wonderful book." "Are you Russian? Are you Orthodox? Do you keep the feast of the Transfiguration?" "No, I am
Anglican. By our calendar we have already kept the Transfiguration, but I know that for you it is in a day or two. I think
you said the Cathedral of the Transfiguration is working (as a
church). Where is it?" "In Pestel Street. I'll show you."

If you ask the way to a church, the most frequent answer is
"Don't ask me I am young. Ask the old women. They know".
But a largish minority not only know and tell you carefully how
to go, but also generally convey that they wish they could go
with you.

One man was from Odessa, where the Germans had hanged
the whole of his family. The fear of war goes right down the age
scale. Even those born after the war grew up in its shadow,
without their fathers or brothers, and sometimes without
mothers or sisters. Apart from the casualties, direct or indirect,
every D.P. in the west means a broken family in the Soviet
Union. A friendly drunk had been twelve when the Germans
overran his home town. Even at that age it was safer to hide,
but one day the Germans came to take his mother for forced
labour in Germany. So he came out of his hiding place and

said, "Take me." His brother had been killed in the war. "I hate all religious people. While my heart beats I will never believe. If there was a God, my brother would not have been killed. And now my son is twelve and the *religiyozniki* are trying to entice him." "But I believe in God." He looked at me in bewilderment and kept saying over and over again, "You are a good man. You use your mind. And you support culture. You are a good man. You use your mind . . ." I took a liking to this man and his friend the retired colonel. If they had been even a little less drunk we might have got quite a long way with our discussion.

A rather older woman said, "I was eight when my father died from typhus in 1920. They brought him home from hospital and in our simplicity we thought they had cured him, but in reality they could do no more for him and in a few days he died. I shall never forget the fever he had the day before he died." And then she worked in a factory during the siege. "We could hardly stand and people fell down dead in the streets but still we did what we could. Nothing was ready. The army were just standing about in the fields. We were supposed to be friends with the Germans. Everything is much better now." I asked her the way to various churches, and later I told her, using the colourless language that one learns to use for all references to tricky subjects, "I have been to all those places you told me of." "I congratulate you. It is very pleasant to be in those places." She has some Poles as neighbours sharing the same flat with her and she thinks it is very wrong that the Churches are separated and even have different calendars. Her neighbours take her to the Catholic church and she takes them to the Orthodox, but she always feels pain when the feasts of the Church come round. "Christ is born twice, and Christ rises twice from the dead but there is only one God, one faith and one baptism."

When I returned from Pskov to Leningrad, I found two West Indian friends standing in the lounge of the Evropeisky Hotel. The husband and I embraced and decided to go to church together, and it being Saturday evening we went to Vespers at the Cathedral. It took three hours, of which I stood through two

and a quarter. Everything in St. Petersburg, and now in Leningrad, was and is that much more European than the rest of
Russia. The eighteenth-century Cathedral of St. Nicholas is
pure rococo, as light as air and with gilt everywhere, like something in Bavaria, but yet Russian and Orthodox. Instead of the
usual chants, music by Rimsky Korsakov was sung by some
magnificent voices. Rimsky's church music seems to lack that
meretricious quality that mars so much of his other work. The
Cathedral was packed, which means thousands rather than
hundreds, and practically no-one left before the end, though one
has to stand all the time. The concentration was terrific. How
they sang the congregational parts! Over and over again we had
that beautiful hymn about the Blessed Virgin Mary ending
"incomparably more glorious than the Seraphim, who without
corruption borest the Word of God, thee truly the bearer of
God do we magnify". Each time they sang it penetrated deeper,
and then suddenly it stopped. My West Indian friends got into
the groove at once; the wife said, "This is life to them; going to
church is not something extra that they do."

The next day we went to the Baptist church, which is now in
the outer suburbs, forty-five minutes' tram ride from the centre,
and then a walk. The convenient central church I remember
from former visits has been taken away and they have been
given a building in this inconvenient place. It is a former
Orthodox church but they have Baptisised it successfully by
painting it blue-grey all over, taking out the iconostasis and
seating the Presbyter and his entourage where the sanctuary
was, facing the people. My friends, who come from the high
church Methodism of the Caribbean, knew most of the hymns
and sang them lustily. They said they are mostly hymns that are
to be found in the Methodist hymn book, but are not sung now,
belonging as they do to the Moody and Sankey era. Here again
they felt quite at home. "They are just like the hill people in
Jamaica."

The service seemed slightly more dry and set than usual, but
there was a clear need for discipline; and how can you have
discipline without being set? As in Pskov the congregation took

turns to lead in prayer, but one old man went on too long.
Presbyter interrupted him with a hymn and then continue
prayer himself, but the old man got his own back with a bar
of counter-prayer. The sermon was on church discipline and
love within the Church. Scripture was very firm on the neces-
sity of obeying the Church and only the Church could excommunicate. This was a clear reference to the schismatic group
who have purported to excommunicate the rest of the Baptist
Church — a ticklish subject that is too complicated to be
expounded here. Some brothers who had been excommunicated
were going round working up sympathy from people who did
not know the whole circumstances. At this there were some
knowing nods.

The next day was the Transfiguration and, as I approached
the Cathedral of that dedication, I could see lights from far
down the street. There were crowds outside the church door and
one could feel the excitement from a considerable distance. The
crowd was so thick that I thought I might have to stay outside
as I have seen people do at Easter, but eventually we all fought
our way inside. Considering this was a working day, it was
remarkable how many men of working age were there. A few
students looked like our own boys. It is hard to estimate the
degree of risk they were running of being expelled from the
University and having their careers ruined, but they certainly
ran some risk through being seen in church; no doubt spies
were present, but they can't identify everyone and even police
spies can sometimes turn a blind eye. There had been an earlier
celebration at seven and no doubt many people had gone to that
before work, as I have seen them do in Odessa.

It was hopeless to try and get to the front — and I am a good
pusher — but eventually I got to the middle. On these occasions
one is always being given candles and flowers and lists of people
to be prayed for, with instructions about which altar they are to
go to. Someone taps you on the shoulder and whispers "To the
Saviour", "For the Festival" or "To the Virgin who is Quick to
Hear", or whatever it is. You look around, tap someone in front
of you on the shoulder and pass the message on.

The sermon began by asking why some people do not get much out of going to church. The answer was "lack of concentration". "You don't listen. And don't say you cannot understand Slavonic. Russian and Slavonic are very close to each other, and, if you listen carefully, you will find that you can understand nearly everything, even if you are quite uneducated." This is true. Indeed simple people often understand Slavonic better than people who are brought up on a modern vocabulary. But one needs patience. At first I could understand very little of what went on in Orthodox churches.

After the sermon there was a *krestny khod*, a procession bearing the cross round the church. These processions used to be a great feature of church life but nowadays they are generally prevented on the ground that they "interfere with traffic", whether there is any traffic or not. But this church stands in its own grounds, so that there is no question of that. As we were swept to the door the bells beat wildly—for a church to have its own bells left is an exception. I kept on tripping up over various obstacles and wondered whether I should be trampled to death, if I fell. But there was no question of falling; the crowd was too tightly packed. Back in church there was great excitement as the cross was lifted up for us to see. Then there was more singing, and speeches began. But that was enough for me and I started a weary walk to get some lunch eventually at half-past three. I sat by a Yugoslav student who was furious at the offhand way the restaurant treated him, as well he might be. He said the Russians were intensely interested in Yugoslavia and were always asking him about the freedom they have there and how it is combined with socialism.

I strolled into the Nevsky Prospekt and visited Gastronom Number One, the delicatessen shop which is still called by the name of its pre-Revolution proprietor, Eliseyev. It remains a period piece with *art nouveau* stained-glass windows. The stuff on sale looked enticing and the girls behind the counter were smarter than usual; one of them was sophisticated and wore fashionable ear-rings. This made me hope that people with some ambition are beginning to go into services. In the past

Soviet shop girls have too often been those who could get no other job. Indeed all services were despised and neglected. Production alone counted. And where shortage was universal all goods were snapped up in a minute. So the ablest people went into production, with the consequence that services were very badly organised, if indeed they were not altogether lacking. This, however, is changing. Shops are still inefficient but some attempt at salesmanship is now made. And one sees dry-cleaners, watch-repairers, cobblers and the like in numbers that are much better than they were, even if they are not yet sufficient for the needs, and not always efficient. I have been warned against the dry-cleaners. At any rate it no longer takes a wangle to get one's shoes mended. At one time you could hardly get spare parts for anything without bribery or influence and, when you got a spare part, it was often stolen or the product of unauthorised cannibalisation. Now there are special departments in shops for the spare parts of bicycles, etc.

I dwell on these matters for a special reason. There are two rough indicators for watching the Soviet Union's social and political progress, the growth of services, which includes repairs and the supply of spare parts, and the growth of a sense of law. Under Stalin, to demand your legal rights was useless; if authority did not spontaneously give what you were entitled to, any complaint was a complaint against authority and that was very near to treason. Even now it takes civil courage to insist on one's legal rights, and there are recent instances of people being severely punished simply for asking that the law should be applied. But more and more those who are aggrieved are beginning stubbornly to claim their legal rights, whether they are writers, scientists, members of the Orthodox or Baptist Churches, Ukrainians or Crimean Tartars, to mention a few recent instances.

The tourists, who now come in shoals to Moscow and Leningrad and certain other places, may or may not understand what they are seeing, but in either case they are becoming a factor in Russian evolution. In the great cities Soviet youth watches the western students carefully and then decides what is worth copying; one thing that has seemed worth imitating is their clothes. Nowadays many young Russians are beautifully dressed in the modern style. Their skirts are short, though not *mini* as the King's Road judges these things. And ways of behaviour go with style of dress. The Russian boys and girls are still more inhibited than ours about showing their affection in public but their public behaviour becomes less conformist every year. Stalinism depended on strict conformism and even on drabness. To be in the slightest way singular was to ask for trouble. It might be too much to say that, now Stalin is gone, new styles in dress go with new styles of thought. But it is the well-dressed, those whose clothes express their personalities, who will make the free Russia of the next generation. The Russian revolutionaries of the nineteenth and twentieth centuries were frumps. Those who are now making a new Russia are anything but frumps.

But this is a digression. My immediate objective was to get to Novgorod. And at last one evening I found myself in the train on the way there; it was a far cry from the pre-revolutionary rolling stock made in Belgium, that did duty not so many years ago. I sat in a smart, up to date, open plan carriage with comfortable seats rather like aeroplane seats. A woman in white overalls went up and down before we started, selling *crème brûlée* ice and warning us that it would be more expensive later in the evening. She did good trade; Soviet ices are much better than any but the most expensive English ices, but Soviet *crème brûlée* ice has nothing to do with the sweet of that name as served at Trinity College, Cambridge.

When we arrived at eleven o'clock at night, I felt thirsty and went to the hotel restaurant. It was smaller and much less smart than the restaurant at Pskov, but people were enjoying themselves and there was some pretty good flirting. If you wanted music, you brought your transistor.

I got up the next morning to see people quietly sitting in the sun on benches at the back of a five-storey block of flats, where there was a nice open space. Somehow one never used to see that sort of thing. People never seemed to have time to just sit.

The young and middle-aged were at work and the old were standing in queues for them.

Novgorod had grown three times over, since I was last there, but it is still quite a small town. It was badly knocked about in the war and has had to be entirely rebuilt, except for the oldest parts. The best of the new buildings are undistinguished and the worst are frightful, but most of them are to scale and there are plenty of parks and gardens and a fun-fair. The Kremlin is the equivalent of an English cathedral close. Just beyond it is a beautiful sandy beach with kiosks and people bathing, where the famous bridge of Novgorod used to stand. Some East Germans were laying a wreath on the monument to the defenders of Novgorod in the last war. I found they were nice people when I got to know them afterwards, but I wondered what they were thinking as they laid the wreath. The Russians told me what they thought and you can guess what it was. Some Germans who fought here come back as tourists, which is not well received.

After breakfast I went into the Intourist bureau to arrange sight-seeing. I had only one day and they told me that I was welcome to look at the outsides of buildings but everything was shut for the day. This was not good enough but it took the whole morning and I had to pull every string I knew, including a telephone call to Leningrad, before I could arrange to stay an extra day.

In Pskov there is a continuity of life from the mediaeval republic to the present day, but in Novgorod the chain has snapped. Once the power of republican Novgorod extended to the Urals and the Arctic Ocean. "Who can stand against God and Lord Novgorod the Great?" In such phrases the power of the great merchant city was personified, as the Honorable East India Company was later personified as John Company. Pskov, the "younger brother of Novgorod", played Moscow's game and was spared. Novgorod was broken by Ivan the Terrible and after that never became more than a Russian Barchester. And then she was broken again in the second world war when the fighting line passed through the middle of Novgorod and half her ancient monuments were destroyed.

I was travelling light, having left my main luggage at Leningrad, and had only one pair of trousers, the seat of which suddenly split. What to do? Fortunately the second or third rate hotel I was staying at had a cobbler and a sewing woman permanently in attendance to cope with these emergencies. The sewing woman was a jolly person in her forties and she did rather a rough repair in a trice. I asked her where there was an open church. She laughed and said she did not know, but told me the general direction. "Are there churches open in England?" I was asked this several times in Novgorod, which is one of the things that showed me that the Church is in much worse case in Novgorod than in Pskov. On consulting the record later, I found that out of at least fifty-five churches open in the diocese of Novgorod a few years ago, only five are open now. I have described elsewhere the mixture of force and fraud by which the churches are closed in the Soviet Union. In this case the relentless pressure of the Soviet authorities was greatly aided by the supineness of the bishops.

Until a few years ago a largish, suitable church in the centre of the town was in use but it has now been turned into a planetarium. They said the bell kept people awake. Now the only "working" church is a small one on the outskirts which either has no bell or is not allowed to ring it. There was a young priest with a small congregation for evensong. Distances are quite big in Novgorod and public transport was little use. So I walked, about ten miles each day. Unfortunately I had dysentery and was often tired and sometimes faint.

On the second day I overcame my tiredness and got ready by nine, as I was told, for a long day's sight-seeing. But nothing was ready, no guide, no car, and it would cost fifteen roubles to have a car for all I wanted to see. That was too much, so I said I would walk and they must find me a guide who could walk. Most of the Russian girls have very strong legs, the legs of those who are accustomed to walking far. Then all the places I wanted to see were shut, all the keepers being at a meeting, and no-one knew how to get the keys. And as for the church of the Spas na Iline, with the world famous frescoes by Feofan Grek, which above all things I wanted to see, it was one excuse after another. "It is shut for repairs." "But perhaps it could be specially opened for me. I am, after all, the Treasurer of the Great Britain–U.S.S.R. Association." "It is only for specialists." "I am a specialist." "It is dangerous." "I will risk that." "You will not be able to see anything. It is covered with scaffolding." "I will climb the scaffolding." "You will not need permission to see it. The people who are working there can let you in." "But you said they couldn't." And so on. It was a running fight for most of the day. Never have I worked so hard to see anything, as on my two visits to Novgorod.

Eventually, about ten, I set off in a car to see the first sight and to try to find the guide, a man who lived nearby. The first sight was shut and the guide was in bed. But I did not particularly want to see the sight, and the guide got up. We got into one church, with the help of the keeper's husband, she being at the meeting. "It is always easier to get round a man." I saw at once that the best things were up beyond a cord saying "No Entry". The guide said, "It is dangerous." But I said, "There is no danger whatever." And, before he could do anything, I was well on my way up. After that they were on my side and would do anything to get a church open. We tried the Spas na Iline and shouted to the restorers working inside, but without result. Later in the day they told me they never answered the door; otherwise they could not get on with their work. The co-operative driver somehow got the key to the church of the Nativity of our Lady at the Cemetery and we went there. The restorers knew a trick worth two of that, they had put their own padlock on the door. But we pulled the staples right out and got in. It was very dark but I saw something.

In the end we got a promise from one of the girls at the Museum to take me to the Spas herself, if I would come at four o'clock in the afternoon. She was half an hour late but it was worth waiting. We climbed the ladders, lay flat on our backs right under the dome and saw many wonderful things. These frescoes, or some of them, are reproduced in all the books and, if you have seen them, you will remember that Feofan seems to have used an extraordinarily coarse brush. I imagined that, when one saw the originals, much more detail would be visible. But no. There is nothing to see but those broad, bold brush strokes which come out in any good reproduction. But the colour is a surprise. I had imagined that one would see some of the bright Byzantine colours of Feofan's panel painting of the Dormition in the Tretyakovsky Gallery at Moscow but when he came to do these frescoes, reddish-brown and white were the colours. Almost a Rembrandt of the fourteenth century, *mutatis mutandis*. There was far more originality, individuality and local variety in the Russian middle ages than you would ever guess from reading the literature of the period. Before the nineteenth century the Russians seemed unable to write. Their genius was expressed in architecture and in painting, most of which is for practical purposes still largely inaccessible. So certain periods of Russian culture remain greatly under-estimated. The usual view is that the years of "the Tartar Yoke", the later middle ages, were a time of regression and that Russia only recommenced her slow climb with the establish-ment of the centralised monarchy in Moscow at the end of the fifteenth century. I used to accept this but one penetrating critic, the late G. P. Fedotov, thought the period of the Tartar Yoke was in many ways a greater time than the Muscovite period, which succeeded it, and which in his view was a time of regression in various most important respects. I am beginning to think that he was right.

My guide on this occasion was a local girl who had taken up the study of Novgorod's past and become enthusiastic about it. She showed me that extraordinary painting of St. Makarius with his long, white beard coming down to the ground and covering him, done in Feofan's strongest impressionistic style and said, "It is from the Bible. He taught Hesychast prayer," (the Jesus prayer, i.e. the concentration of "the mind in the heart" through the perpetual repetition of the publican's prayer, offered in the name of Jesus, "Lord Jesus Christ, son of God, have mercy on me a sinner"). She would hardly believe that Makarius was not in the Bible. "But he was one of the desert

father." "Yes, in the Bible." "Oh no! That isn't in the Bible."
"Really, are you sure?" "Yes, quite sure." Russians never
could distinguish between Scripture and other holy writings.
"And you know about the Hesychasts?" "Yes." "That is very
hard for a young person to understand. It seems to abstract you
from life." "Not necessarily."

By degrees she got so enthusiastic about showing me things
that she insisted on taking me to see the church of the Nativity
of our Lady at the cemetery. I did not dare say that I had
already broken into it that morning. So we started a long walk
outside the walls to the very pretty cemetery with trees growing
thick over the graves and wrought-iron railings round each family
burial place, with a little wooden bench to sit on when one
visits the resting place of one's departed. On the way we met a
fair-haired boy of eighteen. "What are you doing, Alyosha?" "I
am looking at antiquity." "So are we. Come along." This time
we had a proper key to get in with and Alyosha turned the
lights on, so that we could see properly.

The authorities cannot make up their mind how to handle
the religious art of the past. Sometimes they show it as part of
Russia's glorious heritage and sometimes they try to stop you
seeing things in case they should put non-Marxist ideas into
your head. In museums the icons are a perpetual reminder of a
mystery that refuses to vanish. What do people make of them?
They look carefully but they do not say much. It is interesting
to listen to the guide lecturers. They and the restorers are people
who have been drawn to icons for various reasons, aesthetic or
otherwise. I never ask questions but I could see that questions
arise spontaneously about the deeper meaning of what the
icons represent and that there are animated conversations on
this subject between trusted friends. More than once I have
heard the guide lecturers give what was in effect an admirable
theological lecture on the meaning of a particular icon. St.
Nicholas was no Father Christmas but a real historical character who had played a prominent part in the history of the fourth
century. His miracles, if you considered them carefully, were
not supernatural, but rather expressions of the highest Christian

morality, which was fully in accordance with "our Communist morality". In the famous miracle of the storm, it was St. Nicholas who took the tiller. The "mythical iconography of the crucifixion" had become fixed in the sixth century; and of course there *is* a mythical element in the iconography—the skull of Adam, for instance. I asked whether there was any historical foundation for the legend of St. Parasceva. "It is disputed. She was reputed to have been martyred under Diocletian but the earliest extant life is of the seventh century." "That sounds fishy." "But there may have been earlier lives lying behind the version that we have." This was interesting since in writing it is Soviet policy to refer to "the mythical Christ" and I have been asked by educated people whether he really existed. Suggest that religion belongs to the land of myths and fairy tales and people will cease to believe—or will they?

The country, the river and Lake Ilmen are a very real part of Novgorod's life. One afternoon I went for a cruise on a hydrofoil, Russia's answer to the hovercraft, and very smooth and pleasant it was, though a bit noisy. We shot past beautiful monasteries and very sad ruins, relics of the last war, out into the pure waters of Lake Ilmen, just as it was in the days of Sadko, the twelfth-century merchant of Novgorod who became a fairytale figure. People were fishing happily in their little boats, too intent to give us a wave. It was hazy and at one moment we were entirely out of sight of land. As well as the hydrofoil there are plentiful pleasure steamers on the Volkhov, and if it had not been for my dysentery, I would have booked myself for a "gay evening" on board, returning at eleven p.m.

I made friends with one man who had travelled, and even lived, abroad but likes Novgorod best. "In the autumn my wife and I go collecting mushrooms and berries. We have already made enough jam for the whole winter. I am very lucky and my wife's grandmother has three plots of land in her village. I help her to work them. She keeps bees and I get plenty of honey. I love fishing and go out in my motor boat on Lake Ilmen as often as I can. Nearly everyone has a motor boat."

Only a few years ago the Russian villages, where nearly half

the people still live, seemed to be dying. The young and ener-
getic left for the towns, if they could, to escape the desperate
poverty and gloom of rural life after Stalin. The new régime
had exploited the peasants with even less mercy than the land-
lords and the Tsar in the old days. In the war I once listened to
some peasants discussing the past. It was common ground that
under Stalin things were worse than ever before. It was a moot
point whether life had been better under the Tsar or "under
Lenin". Relics of serfdom still remain; the peasants are not
formally "bound to the soil" but equally they are not given
internal "passports" like other citizens. This can make it very
difficult for them to get work anywhere, except at their place
of birth. The word *kolkhoznik* or collective farmer is pronounced
with the same overtone of contempt as the old *moujik*. Now,
however, the terms of trade have been dramatically changed in
favour of the peasants, so that they are at last able to earn good
money; and they can always find something to spend it on,
when they go to town, even if the village shops still remain bare
and primitive. I kept on hearing: "Four years ago the peasants
did not know what oranges or washing-powder were. Now they
come in and buy them by the crate, or several crates at a time.
We go in and find that the peasants have bought up everything." This last being said in an aggrieved tone, the way some
people might speak in London, if they went into Fortnum and
Mason and found they could not buy any crystallised fruit,
because the Jamaicans had bought it all up, or in New York if
the Puerto Ricans had done so. "They are even overcoming
their feeling of social inferiority and have no shame in coming
into the best restaurants in their peasant clothes. They have
money and they show it. People are afraid of them, when they
come into a restaurant." One day I sat at table in a smart
hotel with a very *jungly* man from Uzbekistan; he had got into
the part of the restaurant that was supposed to be reserved for
foreigners, though he could hardly speak Russian or anything
but Uzbek. With his swarthy face, his rough features and his
grubby clothes he seemed a typical Turkestan peasant from an
age that went back to Tamberlaine and long before. Obviously

he had come to Moscow with money, and obviously he had come to make more money, and he drank vodka as if it was light table wine. I heard conservatives complain, "The peasants buy all sorts of things that are no use to them, like pianos and fridges." And, "They have brought in a money-grubbing ideology, and that is one of the things that makes life sordid nowadays. It has spread to everyone. The peasants have no interest in culture or international affairs."

All this may be so, but what does one expect? The peasants have been exploited for so long that it is hardly surprising if they now try to get their own back, and if at first their table manners are uncouth.

It is only fair to add that the very same people who said these snobbish things about the peasants were also the first to say, "The rural intelligentsia have changed out of all recognition. Nowadays peasants can go straight to college from their villages and then go back when their education is finished." The hope is that they will stay in the villages and take the place of the petty functionaries from the towns who have been an alien, and sometimes hated element in the countryside.

All this could change Russia radically, if it comes to fruition. One reason why Russia has never been on an even keel since the Revolution is that no educated person has been willing to bring his children up in the countryside. The civilised country life of Chekhov's day had collapsed and nothing had taken its place. But now the renewed interest in orchards and gardens, and in other country pursuits is joining with the prosperity of the peasants to make the villages, or some of them, places worth living in. It is now not uncommon for people to prefer the country to the town. The Russian peasants may have rough manners but they will learn how to eat properly with a knife and fork and many other things, as soon as they are given a chance.

How general is the peasant prosperity? My Russian friends usually said it was general all over the country. "Why, I have just come back from the far east and I found the same there. The trappers round Lake Baikal now get a fair price for skins and this has killed the black market" — an obvious exaggeration that, but no doubt there is less of a black market in fur. "The peasants are rich now. And yes, it is quite true what you heard. The peasant houses in this part of Siberia are all different from each other, and all beautifully carved with fret-work patterns like lace; and nowadays they are all beautifully painted." But foreigners in Moscow generally said that, though the general improvement was enormous, there were parts of the country which were still pretty poverty-stricken. Both Russians and foreigners agreed that far too little is being done to make even tolerable country roads. While this remains so, it stands to reason that those villages which lie off the main lines of communication will remain poor. My Russian friends were reporting truthfully what they had seen, and they had travelled widely, but perhaps they had not been into the remote "bears' corners", which still abound. The Russians do not know all of their country. Even party officials appointed to supervise the countryside do not generally penetrate to the really remote places.

Yet, all in all, there is now far more hope for the Russian villages than at any time in the last forty years.

CHAPTER VIII

Moscow

I never knew the old Moscow, the "big village" that was so
unlike half-European St. Petersburg. When I first saw Moscow
the "forty times forty" churches that adorned the "old capital"
had mostly been pulled down. But the long, low stucco houses
with their Doric columns built after Napoleon's fire in 1812
still dominated over wide areas. The city had hardly grown
since before the Revolution and the new population that flowed
into the capital was crowded into the old buildings whose
stucco had begun to peel and their roofs to leak. The crowding
was not worse than the worst of Moscow before the Revolution,
it may even have been not quite so bad; but in the old days
overcrowding had been exceptional; now it became general. It
was some compensation that fields, forests and marshes lay just
outside the city's modest bounds and one could take a couple of
rooms as a *dacha* in one of the villages near Moscow with a little
river, as yet unpolluted, and a good suburban train service. In
Moscow itself a family was glad to have a whole room to itself in
some flat that had been built for a bourgeois family before the
Revolution. The kitchen and "usual offices" would be shared by
several families, who generally managed to live together without quarrelling. In one case that I knew two families shared a
smallish flat. In the kitchen there was a gas stove with four rings;
each wife had two rings and considered herself well off. Sometimes you see a row of fridges side by side in a kitchen.

In those grim last years of his life, from 1948 to 1953, Stalin
began to pull down old Moscow apace and to replace the old
buildings with monstrous skyscrapers built to his own specifica-
tion. Wedding-cake-like imitations of the Kremlin towers were
erected on rectangular boxes. The famous view of Moscow from

the Lenin Hills (formerly the Sparrow Hills) across the river became ugly. The Kremlin which had long ruled supreme over this once lovely scene became scarcely noticeable among all the enormous banality. But this hideous new building had made no appreciable difference to the dreadful overcrowding; the official statistics showed that. After Stalin's death in 1953 his successors began to take the provision of housing more seriously, but inevitably it took two or three years before the new policy was both formulated and put into effect.

Many Soviet towns now have a series of concentric rings. In the centre is the old city, whatever that was like. Outside it is a ring consisting of blocks of flats built in a great hurry in the years after 1956. They all look as like as two peas and are large, plain and ugly; the flats are very small and not well designed. But the policy was right. After more than a generation of neglect something had to be done quickly and there was no time for refinements. At last those ghastly cellars into which people were heaped began to empty and even the millions of people return-ing from concentration camps were absorbed without too much strain. As time went on it became possible to build better and the next ring of buildings, put up in the early 'sixties, is an enormous improvement. Better designed and less cramped. If at the end of the nineteen-fifties Moscow made London look like a museum of good architecture, within a few years Mos-cow's current architecture had improved so much that, if the improvement had continued, London would soon have been left behind. At that point Moscow got stuck and most of the current architecture is very ordinary. As one drives out of Mos-cow one passes miles of conventional contemporary façades. The swanky decoration that Stalin favoured has gone, but the proportions of the buildings now in vogue are very common-place and, if one may believe the Soviet press, there is still very much bad workmanship. The average Muscovite now has about seven square yards of floor space. Layout however continues to improve.

During my last visit I spent day after day travelling from end to end of what is now a vast city, trying to find people I had known before. At one time people crowded into "the centre", which is a definable and small area. If you take a taxi in the suburbs you say, "To the centre", and it is only later that you say which part of the centre you want to go to. Twenty years ago everyone lived in the centre if he could, but a few years ago my friends started saying, "The centre has lost its attraction." Many people preferred to live in the suburbs. And I can see why.

Kuntsevo is my favourite suburb. You go to the end of the underground line and then you take a bus for miles and miles. I began to be anxious about overshooting my stop and my fellow passengers decided to tease me about it. "Oh, it's thirty-five kilometres. It will take you an hour and a half." Then, when my face fell, they laughed and said, "We will tell you where to get out, if you will tell us who you are." So I told them. "We all have a very high opinion of the English"—they call us all English whether we are Scots, Irish or Welsh—"but now the Americans, that is another matter." "I don't much like the American social system myself but the Americans are good people." "Well, I can't understand it. I suppose you saw the T.V. programme last night?" "No. What happened?" "They showed some American airmen who had been captured in North Vietnam and asked them why they bombed women and children, and they answered, 'It is our work. We are paid for it.' Now that is a very funny attitude to work." "Yes, a very funny attitude. And it is not the American attitude. I don't know where they got those airmen from." A quick look. And a change of subject. They had learnt what they wanted and no one had said anything that he shouldn't.

At Kuntsevo everyone said, "Can you smell the country air? There are mushrooms in the woods not far from here." At this time of year one seems to hear a conversation about mushrooms every day; the Russians are great experts in this matter and think it very strange that we only eat *shampinyony*. Beside the surburban streets wild flowers were growing eighteen inches high and a mother was showing them carefully to her tiny son. I had never realised before how the Russians loved flowers. At both Pskov and Novgorod there had just been flower shows and on every hand I saw evidence of this love of flowers. This was not always so. At one time the Soviet people seemed like a certain Mr. Bogdanowicz who, when flowers were put in his room, said, "I have no time for them." But now they were beginning to enjoy "eating the air", to use the Indian phrase. And Kuntsevo stands on dry, sandy soil where the pine-scented air is worth eating. The architecture is dull but the layout is excellent. Uniform oblong boxes of five stories with no pretensions whatever were universal but the distances between them and the angles were right, so that one got the benefit of a half rural setting; and the place was on a human scale. After an evening at Kuntsevo we took a taxi back to the centre; one rouble and fifty kopeks for eleven miles; not bad.

The next day I went to the other end of the city, which had the same general character but was less pleasing. Few foreigners penetrate to the suburbs by public transport, and my advent caused interest. In the centre you may see that set expression even on the faces of children of twelve, but here I thought people were less conscious of being watched. They were certainly in less of a hurry and more ready to see me on my way. No buses took me very near where I wanted to go, since the direct route lay across a bridge that was being reconstructed. But a boy of about eighteen took me in hand and led me by back paths through the gardens between the houses. It had rained a little and was muddy; in the autumn rains and the spring thaw these paths must turn into a quagmire. "I will show you the way, but the name of the street and the number of the house have both been changed. That's Number 15 now. I should try these first. The old Number 15 is that block on the right." It turned out that the official inquiry bureau had given me the new number but the old name of the street. I skirted the untidy back of a long straggling block of about seven stories and eventually found the right number. Russian addresses can be very complicated. You have to know the street number, the number of the subsidiary block, and the number of the flat; and it is useful to know the number of the entrance and what floor it is on.

One generally gets detailed instruction how to proceed after locating the right number. On this occasion I knew that the man I was looking for was married, but the only thing I knew about his wife, Tanya, was that she had one leg. I knocked and was reassured by a thumping sound, as of a wooden leg. In a minute the door was opened by a grey-haired little woman with a serene face, walking on crutches with no artificial leg. I explained who I was, and she seized my hand with a beaming smile. "We must go at once to find Alyosha before he leaves his work. It is not far." But it took an hour with several changes of bus, trolley-bus and tram, and when we got there Alyosha had gone. Tanya moved about with amazing agility on her crutches. She knew just how to leap onto a tram with one leg. She talked unceasingly and I found her to be one of those splendid people, who gave the Party its soul in the days when it had a soul, one of those idealists who carry one back to the simpler 'thirties when black was black and red was white. She believed that Hitler only persecuted the Jews if they were poor or proletarian, and that he protected rich Jews. But when she spoke of her own family, her talk was wise and kind. She could retire now and live on a pension but she works hard, organising nature study in all the schools in one of Moscow's vast *rayons* (boroughs). Afterwards, when I described Tanya as a real political idealist, the comment was, "Really! There are not many of them left now."

It was dark when I got home and a grandfather was waiting with his little grandson at the bus stop. "Look at that lovely moon." "Where?" "In the clouds over there." A pause, and then contemptuously, "That's not the moon." "What is it, then?" "That's cosmic space." "And I thought it was the moon."

In the last seventeen years of Stalin's rule it was rare indeed to get inside anyone's flat, though even then it could be done. Now people ask you home without much constraint. I do not know the habits of the real bigwigs, who still live a secluded life that is said to be luxurious. The late Alexis Tolstoy, as a successful writer, was a rich man with a smart flat in Moscow and a *dacha* in the country that would have been a credit to a moderately successful Surrey stockbroker. That is the nearest I ever got to the real upper crust. But even the Soviet flats that I know are very various. They belong chiefly to the middle-ranking members of the educated classes.

You may find yourself in what is unmistakably the diminished drawing-room of a *grande dame* of the old school, or in a flat in an old house that is done up in the contemporary style with curtain material specially brought from London or Paris, or perhaps in a tiny flat built after 1956, and furnished with good modern Scandinavian furniture and ornaments from Estonia. Or you may go into an old house, where even after several visits it may baffle you to draw a ground plan or to say who lives there and in what rooms; but you are likely to find that the people are living well. There may be plenty of room or you may find people doubling up, with signs that a relative sleeps on a couch outside the bed alcove, which may be curtained off. With great good temper the Russians have shared flats for fifty years but now they have had enough sharing and one of the blessings of the new flats is that one can hope to have one's own kitchen and bathroom. One hears, "My neighbours are very nice and they are always doing kind things for me, but their children break all my china. I would love to have some nice china, but it would last no time. And they are dirty."

Sometimes the amenities are less. Once I sat for hours wondering what it was that made the flat I was in so unmistakably Soviet. I thought it was the rough, offhand character about everything. The stairs were made of rough concrete which cracks and flakes off, so that you can easily slip and you can never get it shining clean. The rooms seemed to have been carved in a hurry out of a cube without much regard for shape or convenience. The floorboards were covered with thick paint and had never been properly planed down. The plastering was rough. And so on. But it served. In the times of greatest shortage the most rough and ready accommodation had to do. But Russia is now past that phase.

Behind the showy thirtyish façades of some of the central

streets you will find a rabbit warren of nondescript buildings. Go up an outside staircase and enter; you will find an interminably long, completely dark corridor about twelve feet wide with flat doors let into the wall on each side; knock on one of the doors and you will find a gas stove with various implements including a tin bath hanging up in a lobby about five feet square. Knock again and you will be let into one of the two rooms opening out of the lobby. It will be a large plain oblong with a small window giving little light at the further end, but the plaster and the woodwork will be rather better finished than in some of the older flats. What could such a building be meant for?

It should be added that there has been a continual improvement in the quality of the fittings over the last few years. The new houses round the Arbat Square are considered a model, in this respect at least, but I heard many complaints about the tall plate-glass blocks that are replacing this old quarter. "What has this got to do with Moscow?" they ask angrily. At first the sparkle of the new buildings, along the Kutuzovsky Prospekt attracted me, but it might just as well be in Toronto or Buffalo and in the end I found the rectangular repetitions wearisome. I was glad to hear the Muscovites complain, for in the past I have thought that they were destroying old Moscow without thought and were too easily satisfied with what took its place. The old stucco houses got a bad reputation because they were allowed to get into bad repair, but they had character, and all that was needed was to put them into proper repair and to wait for new building to lessen the overcrowding in the centre. But the Muscovites are still pulling down their old buildings without consideration, except for too few that are considered of historical interest. They will not listen when you tell them they are destroying something Russian and unique, but they will be sorry when they have done it.

For a very long time the shortage of housing made people immobile. If you had somewhere to live, you held on to it, and one still finds people who have lived in the same house since before the Revolution. Sometimes you find people sitting at the same desk after thirty years. Nowadays the best way to get a new flat is to put yourself down as a member of a housing co-operative. It is easy to get land on the outskirts and the block will probably go up quite quickly; but, if you want to stay in the centre, there may be quite a long wait before your co-operative gets a site to build on.

In the streets there are endless little booths where they answer your inquiries, sell you snacks, shine your shoes and mend them, too, if they have time, sell newspapers, and provide a hundred and one small services. These booths are largely made of glass and they get dreadfully hot in summer, like Corbusier's one building in Moscow, the Ministry of Light Industry. In winter they are heated by little electric stoves and are said to be quite warm, but once I had my shoes cleaned by a nice old woman in a booth that seemed to have no possibility of heating. "Do you come here in the winter?" "Yes." "Isn't it cold?" "Yes, very cold." "Why is there no electric stove?" "It wouldn't be any use. This place is so small that I can't work without opening the door."

Another shoe cleaner had a large booth with double glass and was doing a good trade selling shoe laces, iron heel tips and that sort of thing, and doing some small repairs. His girl friend came up and asked, "What is that building?" "It's the hostel for the Bolshoy Ballet, but people like Maya Plisetskaya moved out of it long ago. She has a flat with six rooms." Gasp of amazement. "And her mother has a flat equally large." "What! You can understand Maya Plisetskaya. But her mother!" At that point I joined in and Plisetskaya's flat had soon grown to eight rooms. "But Academicians" — members, that is, of the Academy of Sciences — "only have three rooms. Of course she has a world reputation but so do they." It ended quizzically with, "Well, it seems that ballerinas get more than Academicians." I wonder.

Socially the most important shops are the chain of Beryozka shops, where you must pay in foreign currency. No questions are asked about how you got your *valyuta*, but there are lawful ways of doing so. If you go abroad, you are given quite a generous allowance of foreign exchange, and when you return you can change some of it back into vouchers that can be used at the Beryozka shops. Your friends will give you four roubles for a one rouble voucher. There is a food shop, a clothes shop, a shoe shop, a drink shop, and so on. At these shops they sell good things at reduced prices; many, but not all of the wares come from abroad.

On ne mange bien qu'a la maison. In people's homes the food is delicious, and the drink can be good, too. *Starka*, vodka matured in the cask, is good and the far-sighted housewife will often lay in a store of ordinary vodka, which she then flavours deliciously with fruit in season, allowing it to stand for a few months before it is drunk. In 1968, however, fruit was scarcer than usual, since transport that should have been bringing fruit from the south was employed in the invasion of Czechoslovakia. But this did not affect local fruit and I was given some first-class strawberry jam, specially made at a *dacha* outside Leningrad. I doubt whether England, the home of strawberry jam, could have done so well. There are some good Soviet wines, the best being some of the Georgian wines, but the Bulgarians make the best wine in the Soviet bloc and this is freely available in Moscow. Armenian brandy is now much exported and has become hard to get. The expensive restaurants vary from good to moderate. The best restaurant is at the park and château of the Yusupov family at Arkhangelskoye near Moscow. There was great interest when I said I had seen the Prince Yusupov who murdered Rasputin. A special dinner was ordered while I admired the exceptionally well-grown birches and pines. The pines had reddish stems like Scotch firs but grew much straighter and the birches were much taller and better grown than our birches. It seems that birches live much longer in Russia. The special lunch consisted of bear and elk. Cold bear and cold elk for the *hors d'œuvre* and hot bear and hot elk for the main course. I had had elk before, but not bear. It was delicious with a delicate taste and an unmistakable loose consistency. Of course I was made to eat too much. For Russian hospitality it is a point of honour to overfeed the guest, and after all the hungry years this is understandable. Now that

Russians can eat their fill every day they tend to get fat, especially the women, which is not surprising since at present bread and potatoes make up two-thirds of their diet. I have never seen so many fat women, but that is a phase that will pass.

The difficulty for a foreigner is to get fed without ruining yourself when you are not invited for a meal. There is quite a good *bistro* near the Moscow Arts Theatre where you can get served fairly quickly and may find yourself sitting beside a lady who looks like a distinguished Edwardian actress, or a couple of young men who might belong to the National Theatre Company in London. But if you go during the rush hour, it is very difficult to get served. And at all times it is difficult to get anything to drink with a cheap meal. I have sometimes been reduced to ordering soup which I didn't want, so as to get some liquid. One day two young men sat down beside me and produced a mineral water bottle. "Did you get that here?" "Of course we got it here." "How?" At this they roared with uncontrollable laughter. "Of course we got it here. It's Moscow water." When I still looked perplexed, they explained, "It's out of the tap." So you have to bring your own water. Even at the smart Metropole Hotel where I was staying, it was difficult to get enough liquid, except from the tap. You could get tea (*chay*) at the very expensive and chi-chi *Russkaya Chaynaya*, when it was open, which was seldom. And you could generally get "juice" but you had to take the juice that was going; at first there was nothing but tomato juice and then for over a fortnight there was nothing but mango juice, unless of course you wanted an expensive bottle of wine.

Sometimes in the centre you sit beside interesting companions. There were many businessmen in Moscow, the ones I saw most being Italian, British and Japanese. "Oh yes, there's lot's of business here but we can't keep up with the Japanese. They study what the Russkies want and then they study what we've got and jump between us." But later I heard another story. "The Japs? They compete all right but we've snitched all the trade from them." One day I had an ice in an outdoor café and two Russian stiffs sat down beside me. "I can't do anything with him. He is right out of control." "You can't do anything with the young nowadays." "I see a band of hooligans in the street. I can't do anything by myself and, if you call the militia, they just laugh at you. They used to use their truncheons, but not now." "Brother, it is too late. There is nothing that you or I can do." It was obvious that these types, and there are a fair number of them, would like a return to strong-arm government. They are the modern equivalent of the Black Hundreds of Tsarism's decline, Russia's far more sinister version of our own Hang, Flog and Censor Brigade, or the Vigilantes of America.

There was no night life. I asked a friend to supper after the ballet, but, it being nearly eleven o'clock, we could get nothing but salad and a glass of tea. The next evening I was with the younger generation and they said that even the special "youth cafés" close at eleven. Apparently Khrushchev issued an edict banning night life in restaurants and that was that. This is a shame, for the Russians love to stay up late talking and there used to be a lively night life. I was told on what ought to have been good authority that a change was being prepared; the mother who told me saw that it was absurd to leave things as they are now, but she was in two minds at the prospect of her darling children staying out to all hours. At present, if you want to go and have a meal late, the only thing you can do is to drive out to the airports where the restaurants stay open later. The laws about drinking and driving are very like the British laws, breathalyser and all. One night after a party a certain young man was driving home very carefully; the police thought it was suspicious that he was driving so slowly down an open road; they pulled him in and he lost his licence for a year.

Soviet boys and girls want to do the same things as youth everywhere, and increasingly they are doing them. They spend their money on clothes and dress very well now. Hair dye is used with much more discrimination in Moscow than in the provinces. Art interests them more than politics, so far, and they can be discerning. Official art is despised. And as for restoration: "Here they restore pictures well and buildings badly. You should see what they have done to the Pokrov na Nerli" — a particularly lovely twelfth-century church — "You used to see stone but now it is all concrete." They showed me a book about Vivien Leigh in Russian and were surprised that I did not put Sir Laurence Olivier quite in the first-class as an actor. "Who then? We saw Paul Scofield as Sir Thomas More in *A Man for All Seasons*. Ah, there was a man who was prepared to die for his idea." To suffer for "your idea" is the *in phrase* in progressive circles to denote noble conduct. Among such people you will hear records of Juliette Greco and the Beatles, as well as Aznavour, Vysotsky and other Soviet favourites. In the Soviet Union a pop singer makes his way by success at local competitions and I was told that there have been stars of fourteen years old, but on the whole it takes more time to make a name than it does in the West. I did not see enough of Soviet students to generalise from my own experience, but those I talked to said that the present generation of students are not at all brainwashed, even if they are only just beginning to take an interest in politics. They certainly don't look brain-washed. What young people, both students and workers like to do at present is to club together and get hold of a car and go for a camping holiday out in the fields and forests. The universal rediscovery of the country must surely go with a rediscovery of some traditional Russian values, and there are not lacking those who say that this is indeed so.

Twenty years ago the Russians used to claim that they had no racial prejudice. But most of them had never seen a black man. Now that is changed. In 1968 the African students used to frequent the buffet of the Metropole Hotel, where I had my breakfast and sometimes other meals. They were too busy with their own world to want to talk much to strangers but I listened to their conversations with interest, when they sat at my table. Sometimes they spoke their own languages, such as Somali, when a group of one nation were together, but the *lingua franca* was Russian, which they spoke extremely well. They were attractive people, extremely intelligent, and well-balanced, and they, too, did not seem in the least brain-washed. I expect that many of them will go far when they get back to their own countries. They seemed to have come to terms with their Soviet environment, and I did not hear them discuss racial problems, but my Russian friends continually raised the question of race in Britain and in America. I answered their questions as honestly as I could, and they argued on the liberal side, much as I do myself, but the conversations always ended with, "There is no doubt that it is a very great problem." I kept on hearing stories of taxi drivers who refuse fares from a black boy with a white girl; and the Russians have now a very rude colloquial word for coloured people. One evening, when I got back late at the hotel, a frighteningly vicious altercation was going on between the hall porter and an African student. The policy of giving economic aid to the countries of the Third World is unpopular. "In 1917 we had no help from other countries. Rather the contrary. But we raised ourselves by our own efforts. Why can't they do the same?"

And the Chinese? They are deeply feared as being too numerous, too industrious, and claiming parts of the Soviet Union. The feeling about the Cultural Revolution is one of utter perplexity, not unlike our own. I have heard it said that the Chinese will sort themselves out in the end, but I have also heard expressions of real pain about the destruction of China's cultural heritage. "When the Chinese were here in large numbers they learnt good Russian quickly and, yes, their personal relations with us were excellent. But they did keep to themselves and, looking back on it, that was a bad sign."

I heard contradictory evidence about the extent of anti-Semitism and also about Jewish discontent. Some said that anti-Semitism was greatly exaggerated and others said that Hitler's anti-Jewish propaganda left traces and that the years after the war were difficult, but now things are good between Jews and Russians. However that may be, it is clearly a distinct disadvantage to be a Jew, and many would say that this is a gross understatement. But the Arabs are even more unpopular than the Jews. The Government's pro-Arab policy in the Middle-East is thoroughly disliked. A pro-Israeli policy would be more popular. One evening at a smart restaurant there was a good band, and the dancing seemed to be going well, but things only began to go in a big way when a Jewish party emerged from an inner room, where they had been having a wedding feast. The band struck up a Jewish dance, the *Freylachs*. Jews and Russians, too, then danced with complete abandon and the band had to repeat it several times over. The best dancer was a pretty little Jewish girl of about seventeen who danced with her father and ended up embracing him, which was part of the dance. Everyone applauded her. As the Jews danced the *Freylachs*, they put all their self-mockery and double bluffing pride into it. The Russians danced squarely without penetrating the meaning.

Social snobbery? In Russia, both now and before the Revolution, snobbery takes the form of respect for position rather than for birth. I noticed that, speaking of their own country, some Russians now refer to "the middle classes". Since my last visit to the Soviet Union, I had inherited a baronetcy and I was curious to see what the Russians would make of this. At first I thought they really were completely indifferent but then I noticed that they were protesting their indifference a little too much and I came to the conclusion that many of them were proud of knowing a genuine "Ser", and I found myself being shown off as an "Anglisky Lord".

One day the conversation turned to homosexuality and I was asked with interest, "Do you have that in England, too?"

CHAPTER IX

Attitudes to Death

Russians of all classes take death naturally. There is none of
that coyness which has crept into the West so insidiously since
the beginning of this century. Death is a fact and there is no
pretence. *The Loved One* and *The American Way of Death* are the
most un-Russian books it is possible to imagine. The Russians
know death too well. The first great war was followed by civil
war, then came famine and typhus, then another great man-
made famine, the liquidation of the kulaks, the Terror, and the
second world war, followed by the second Terror of Stalin's
declining years. But familiarity with death has not bred
contempt.

During the second world war I attended a sort of Communist memorial service to Stanislavsky in the Moscow Arts
Theatre. There was a closed coffin on the stage, draped in a red
flag, and the dead man's colleagues came and said goodbye to
him in set speeches. One heard some of the world's greatest
actors and actresses speaking of their teacher and leader on what
should have been a moving occasion, but the experience was
empty. I was not at that time a Christian believer, but even so it
struck me that Communism has nothing to say about death.
There was no development of a theme such as one gets in the
prayer book service for the Burial of the Dead. In the same way,
to visit the Mausoleum where Lenin lies, and where Stalin lay
for a few years beside him, is for me a disturbing experience
precisely because it has no content.

So death is death, but death is also a mystery, and no
ideology can prevent people thinking about that. The poet
Samuel Marshak, whose children's poems and translations of
Burns and other poetry are deservedly popular, once told me

how he and his wife spent the summer somewhere in Wales just before the first world war. During this time their baby daughter died and they were overcome with grief. Marshak was just getting to know the border ballads and he meditated day and night on *The Wife of Usher's Well*, thinking that it would yield up some secret about death.

> I wish the wind may never cease
> Nor fashes in the flood
> Till my three sons come hame to me
> In earthly flesh and blood.

Marshak's deep emotion comes through in the translation that he made of this wonderful ballad, but he said that no secret was revealed to him.

The Russians love their cemeteries and it seems that some of their funeral customs go very far back into the racial memory, to the time before the Christian faith was in the land. Old Izborsk is a natural stronghold between Pskov and the Pecherskaya Lavra, standing on the border between the Slavs and the Finnish tribes, who are now represented by the Esthonians. Here there is a very ancient graveyard where some flat stones stand with mysterious markings on them, that legend has connected with Truvor, brother of Rurik, the half-legendary founder of the Russian state in the ninth century, more than a hundred years before the conversion of Vladimir. At first this graveyard looks so overgrown that you might think it was deserted, but look closer and you will see that the graves are beautifully kept but that the birch trees grow very thick and cast a deep shade. It seems to betoken some ancient worship of groves as the places of the dead and it reminded me of those lines, again from *The Wife of Usher's Well*:

> It fell about the Martinmas
> When nights are lang and mirk,
> The carline wife's three sons came hame.
> And their hats were o' the birk.

It neither grew in syke nor ditch,
Nor yet in ony sheugh;
But at the gates o' Paradise
That birk grew fair eneugh.

Most Russian cemeteries are overgrown in this way, but
between the trees you will find little family graves, each surrounded by a cast-iron or wrought-iron fence, with just room for
a little bench for members of the family to sit on when they
come to tend the grave and plant flowers around it. Most of the
graves will have crosses but some of the newer ones have red
stars or plain spikes instead of crosses, which makes them look
very forlorn among the beauty of the rest of the scene.

The smartest cemeteries, such as that of the Novo-Devichy
Monastery in Moscow, are more tidy and less beautiful. In 1968
a friend and I went to try and find Ehrenburg's grave there.
When he died, not long before, his funeral was a great event
with enormous crowds. Peace be on him at the last! We looked
once more at the marble statue of Alliluyeva, Stalin's wife, and
Svetlana's mother, who was either killed by Stalin or killed
herself in horror at the discovery of her husband's crimes, and
not even his worst crimes; those were still to come. This
cemetery is now only for the nobs. If any person wants to have a
decent grave nowadays, he has to go far outside Moscow. And
graves have to be re-registered every so often or they become
"No-one's grave" and may be taken by the first comer.

Russian burial customs are more realistic than ours. Each
time you go into a church you are likely to see one or more
coffins standing in the entrance with the waxen faces of the dead
laid out with all the splendour of the Orthodox rites but with no
trace of make-up. The forehead of the dead man or woman is
covered with a band of paper printed with what I take to be by
origin prayers in Slavonic but which have long been elaborated
into an illegible pattern, like many of the inscriptions on
mosques. Flowers will be all around and there may be a candle
in the hand of the deceased.

The funeral service is called "the singing away" and it is

traditionally very important to be sung away. Someone who has not had the burial service sung over him is called "a soul that has not been sung away", but that only takes two words in Russian, *nyeotpyétaya dushá*. All Orthodox services are sung; a "said" service does not exist. When the great poetess, Anna Akhmatova, died she was sung away in style and this was an event that moved all Moscow and all Leningrad for she was known to have been deeply religious, though far from being a plaster saint. In one of her poems, not I think yet published in the Soviet Union, she looks back from her tragic middle-age under Stalin to her youth before the Revolution when she was "the gay sinner of Tsarskoye Selo".

In funeral and memorial services the chief note is the seemingly endless singing of the words *Vyechnaya pámyat*, eternal remembrance, which are sung slowly to a haunting little tune until they seem to become part of you. The relatives come and kiss the corpse goodbye and some of the women may wail rather wildly. If the wailing seems excessive, one of the men will draw her gently aside and try to quiet her. In an earlier generation tears would have been allowed to run their course. When I was learning Russian in the war, I read with my teacher the nineteenth-century writer Nekrassov's great tragic poem *Who Can be Happy and Free in Russia*. I quote once again from one of my war-time letters: "It is a wonderful human account of the old peasant life in Russia; a truly wide and profound poem but at times unbearably terrible and sad . . . When the peasant woman loses her baby son in unbearably tragic circumstances she sings in front of the coffin a most touching little song, of which this is a bald translation:

'Oh! you carpenters, you woodworkers, what sort of a house have you made for my little son? Windows are not cut in it, window panes are not set in it nor stoves nor benches. There are no feather pillows . . . Oh, it will be hard lying for my little Dyomushka. Oh, fearful will be his sleep!'

"My teacher told me that such customs are still alive among the peasants. Her brother married a peasant girl; they lost their child and she would not be comforted but chanted this song to herself over and over again without ceasing, just as in the poem." Anyone who is interested to know what customs lie immediately behind the present Russian practice would do well to consult a long-forgotten book, *Rites and Customs of the Greco-Russian Church* by H. C. Romanoff (Second Edition Rivington 1869 with an introduction by Charlotte M. Yonge). Mrs. Romanoff was an English lady who married a Russian officer about the middle of the last century and spent many years in the smaller provincial towns of the Ural region. She sees the things that are only seen by an observant stranger, being too familiar to be noticed by natives. In her days the lamenting for the deceased sometimes reached a wild abandon, not unlike Irish keening. But Ireland is in many ways like an eastern European country that has for some reason got into the extreme west of Europe. Though I was born and brought up in England, I have often found that my Irish blood and Irish folk memories have helped me to understand eastern Europe.

In Russia a recently dead person is referred to as a "newly presented soul" and special rites are observed for the first forty days after death while the soul is newly presented before the throne of God. If you listen carefully to the lists of people who are being prayed for, you will hear the priest say "newly presented Ioann, newly presented Natalya" and so on. The old Slavonic forms of names are always used in the church services. So Ivan becomes Ioann. Natalya is the full form of the more familiar Natasha and would be used on all formal occasions, whether in the church or in the world.

At certain intervals after everyone dies, and in particular when the first forty days are over, you may see a strange ceremony in church with candles and a sort of cake called *kutiá* made of boiled rice with raisins and sweetened with honey. This is distributed to the guests with biscuits; at least I saw biscuits being handed round on one occasion. The significance of this ceremony is obscure and it seems to be another survival of a pagan rite.

In 1968 I happened to be in Moscow over the time when the Orthodox Church celebrates the anniversary of the Falling

Asleep of the Blessed Virgin Mary. I have described the day of the Dormition at Zagorsk in another chapter, but the whole week was filled with beautiful and symbolic ceremonies of which I attended some but not all. Even for me there comes a limit. But these events made me think much about death and falling asleep. The Orthodox hold no dogma of the bodily Assumption of the Virgin Mary but their liturgies for this season do indicate their traditional beliefs. It is disputed whether there is any difference of substance between the Catholic and the Orthodox beliefs on this matter but there is certainly a difference of emphasis. The Orthodox do not allow you to forget for one moment that Mary passed through the gateway of death before being raised to heaven. I have always been puzzled by these ceremonies and doctrines concerning the blessed virgin but, seeing on this occasion what was done in church, I began to get a clearer idea. In death, Mary followed her son, our Lord, dying a real death but knowing it as a falling asleep from which she was soon awoken by her son, who is always represented in Orthodox paintings as carrying away a tiny figure representing his mother's soul, while the apostles remain weeping round her body.

On the eve of the Falling Asleep I went to evensong at the church in the Obydensky Pereulok, which was said to be frequented by the intelligentsia and there were indeed in the congregation quite a high proportion of obviously well-educated men of all ages. At one point they brought in a symbolic coffin all covered with white flowers and the truth of this moment of falling asleep seemed to be concentrated in that coffin.

CHAPTER X

Attitudes to Religion

The alienation of the Russian intelligentsia from the Church goes back well over a hundred years. After the "first Russian Revolution" in 1905 there was, however, a stirring among the intelligentsia when some former Marxists of the most eminent abilities, such as Berdyaev and Bulgakov, became active members of the Orthodox Church. If the Bolshevik Revolution had taken place ten years later than it did, the Church would have been far more ready for new times. As it was the movement of intellectual renewal, which stems from 1906 and accelerated after the Revolution of March 1917, seemed to be cut off by the Bolshevik Revolution in November of that year before there had been time for it to permeate thoroughly through the Church, or to colour the thinking of more than a comparatively small section of the educated classes. Yet the leaven continued to work in ways that were not obvious. In spite of persecution some priests and some brilliantly gifted laymen continued to think their faith through more or less in secret and often in the murderous setting of Arctic concentration camps. At the same time it slowly became evident that Marxism had failed to provide a substitute for religion. Thus the intelligentsia gradually became aware of a vacuum in their souls.

At the end of the nineteen-fifties I began to notice a faint stirring among them, so faint that I could not have sworn to it. On looking up the diaries of my visits to Russia, I find a record of a few straws in the wind, but so few that they might have been the result of a chance gust or eddy. Subsequent events showed however that the wind was indeed turning and that a great change of spiritual and intellectual climate was in preparation.

By the middle of the nineteen-sixties a part of the intelligentsia began to show a passionate interest in religious answers to the ultimate questions of life. This was a turning to Orthodox values, rather than to the Orthodox Church, which had become compromised in the eyes of many by its subservience to the state, a subservience that may well have been inevitable at one time but became a cause of open suspicion in the relatively free atmosphere of Khrushchev's rule. It would be mistaken to suppose that the Kremlin paid well for the subservience of the hierarchy; in fact the nineteen-sixties have been a period of severe and increasing pressure on organised religion, but the Church has survived as a visible body and services take place in those churches which remain open. And those priests who are known to preserve their inner freedom, are greatly respected. It would be a mistake to think that the people, who speak for the Churches in the Soviet Union on international occasions, always represent the views of most believers.

In spite of pressure, amounting sometimes to persecution, the interest in religion continued to grow among the educated classes—it had always been strong among simple people—and at one time it was fashionable in Moscow to go about with a volume of Berdyaev under one arm and a Bible under the other. This sometimes superficial fashion has passed, but the interest grows. The "Czech events" and the accompanying tendency to re-Stalinise have made the progress of free inquiry take less obvious forms but the links between a section of the intelligentsia and the Orthodox Church are now too strong to be broken. It would be wrong to exaggerate this. The number of people in question may not be large, but some of them are key people.

I now find that friends, who formerly expressed no interest in religion and were sometimes markedly hostile, are now anxious to hear what I believe and why I believe it, though they may be reluctant to show what their own views may be. One evening some friends asked if I had always been a believer. I said "No" and told my story. They listened with deep attention saying from time to time "I understand" or "I fully understand", but making no other comment. Later, however, one of them drew me quietly aside and said he could understand belief in God but he did not see how there could be "life beyond the grave". I explained shortly what I believe and what I suppose about this and we left it at that.

In this sort of conversation there is no noticeable difference of attitude between Party Members and other people. And more often than not there is no difference between Jews and Russians in their attitude to Christianity. This is most remarkable in view of Russia's long anti-Semitic tradition and the natural horror aroused among the Jews by forcible conversions and other forms of gross oppression in Tsarist times. Now there are some notable Jewish converts among the younger priests and among the laity. One Jewish intellectual, whom I had not seen for twenty years, asked what I was doing now. "I edit a quarterly magazine. It's a Christian magazine." "Of course." And this was said though I had not been a believer when he had known me before. At the time when the Bible was in fashion it was particularly the Old Testament books that were read and for a time this aroused an interest in the Jewish religion even among people with no Jewish blood. It seemed from the outside that there might be a convergence between Church and Synagogue on the way, but this phase seems to have passed. When I asked among Christians whether relations with the Synagogue were not now better, they laughed and said, "No. Much worse. Because Jews are now coming into the Church to be baptised."

But there is another side to this. Many Jews are deeply conscious of themselves as Jews, and therefore as not Christians. I tend to meet Russianised Jews who would not think of emigrating to Israel, even if they could, any more than of going to Timbuktu. But there are certainly some whose sympathies are tied up with Israel and who might well go there, if they were allowed, though I suspect that Israel would be for most of them no more than a staging post for New York, London or Paris.

One intellectual, who was very conscious of himself as a Jew, had a Russian Bible on the shelf. When he said he was not religious, I pointed to it and said, "Do you read that?" "Yes."

"And what do you think of it?" "I think one can accept what it says." "In what way then, are you not religious?" "A religious person is one who fulfils the rituals of his religion and has a personal relation of prayer to God. I believe in the Absolute but I never use the word 'God', which is a piece of folklore." "But that does not square with some things in the Bible, which you say you accept." He got in a bit of a muddle and more or less agreed with this, continuing, "If I had a religion, it would be Judaism, because the Jewish conception of God is nearest to the Absolute." This was a man who also had a deep affection for traditional Russian culture with its religious roots, and it was clear that what he wanted to say was more than he knew how to say.

As in the West, the religious instinct sometimes finds expression through *fringy* ideas, the transcendental taking the form of incursions from cosmic space. "Do you think the great Tungus meteorite in Siberia was really a meteorite?" "Oh, I think so." "But you know there is scientific evidence that it was really an atomic explosion from outer space," and they detailed the evidence which I did then remember having read; the supposedly hard-headed Soviet censorship sometimes fails to detect pseudo-scientific charlatans, and there are, for instance, as many crank medicines in Russia as anywhere else. "But do you think that men are descended from apes?" "I have no doubt of it." "But don't you think that the first men might have come from other planets? After all there is reason to think that certain supermen, such as Leonardo da Vinci and perhaps Christ came from outer space. That would account for the virgin birth." I did not think so, but I said nothing, for these were lovable and intelligent people, whose views were sane on every other subject, and they showed that deep-seated honesty which one meets in the best Russians. I did, however, say that without God the fate of man was too bitter to be borne, to which the older generation assented with a sad nod.

At one time I began to think that, when all the smoke is cleared away the Russian Baptists might have become a second national Church, comparable with the Orthodox in their hold

on Russia's heart. But this hypothesis must be discarded. The
Baptists are not the main stream but a wonderful tributary of
clear water. The Russians are patriotic to a fault and their
hearts vibrate to memories of the Orthodox past, even when
one would think they had no knowledge of what Orthodoxy
means. And the Orthodox take one into secret holy places that
seem to be unknown to the Baptists. The Russians feel this in-
stinctively in the Orthodox churches long before they can find
words to express themselves. This is felt by simple and intellectual alike and in the end all the talk of Russian tradition is
about things such as this.

In the last few years fairly obviously, and in less evident ways
for much longer, there has been a continued attempt to redis-
cover the Russian past. At times the Russians seem to want to
know desperately who they are. Recently this has involved a
movement that has been compared with the famous "going to
the people" of nearly a hundred years ago when progressive
boys and girls from good families went into the villages partly
to impart progressive ideas, which turned out to be unwanted,
and partly to make contact with the unspoilt Russian
peasantry, the supposed source of ultimate wisdom. Now the
boys and girls who go for camping holidays in the countryside
are once more rediscovering the Russian villages with their
traditional life centred round the wreck of an Orthodox church
with a beauty that seems just on the point of vanishing. Or is
it? The tension between the church-destroying vandals of the
Party and the older values of Russian village life is portrayed in
a famous passage of Solzhenitsyn.

CHAPTER XI

How Do Our Believers Stand?

Orthodox worship only yields its secrets by degrees. It is not for nothing that the devout Orthodox gladly spend those seemingly endless hours in church. It took me a very long time to take this in and, if at last I begin to understand, I am still not sure how much I can explain. The Orthodox Liturgy is like the Book of Common Prayer in that you may easily say to yourself that it is beautiful and quaint and think that is all there is to be said, yet the longer you know the service, the more you see in it. But the Orthodox services have a richer texture than the Prayer Book; and at first hearing they are harder to understand. Their language is about as different from ordinary spoken Russian as Chaucer's English is from what I am writing now. Moreover everything is sung, and sung words, especially when they are sung by a choir, are always harder to hear than spoken words. Much can be understood with a little practice but much more remains indistinguishable until after many hearings one catches one phrase and then another, till at last everything has fallen into place. The Common, that is to say the invariable parts of the service, first become familiar. The Propers, which change from day to day throughout the Church year, are harder to learn, but on the appropriate days they are sung again and again. For instance from Easter to Ascension Day they sing the great Easter anthem "Christ is risen from the dead, by death trampling death underfoot . . ." in a seemingly endless repetition. People love these songs of the Church so much that you will get a specially large congregation on a weekday evening just before Ascension Day so as to sing this song for the last time that year. Some of the Propers, too, are written up beneath the icons portraying the appropriate subject, and if you browse

round Russian churches reading and looking, you will pick up a
good deal about the Church year and its worship. More often,
however, I notice the beauty of some hymn after puzzling out
its words by ear through many repetitions and then afterwards I
notice that it is written up below an icon that I was looking at.
John the Baptist is always called John the Forerunner and I
have often looked at his icons but it was not until I went to
church on his day and was given a book to follow in that I
realised that this name has a double meaning. He was not only
the Forerunner of the Lord on earth but also in the next world,
where he told "them that are in the grave" that the Saviour
had come.

While the choir sings, the priest will be reciting prayers in a
low voice at the altar. If you are invited to stand inside the
sanctuary you can hear these most beautiful prayers quite distinctly. The main part of the congregation do not hear them but
they are aware of them, as the people are aware of the priest's
"secret" prayers in a traditional Latin Low Mass in the Roman
Catholic Church. The priest's prayers at the altar and the
Propers weave a sort of spiritual polyphony around those words
of the Common which are sung aloud by priest, deacon or
choir. I have sometimes been invited to stand with the choir and
look over their shoulders at their books. In this way one can
follow the Propers word by word, even without the long
practice of a hardened Russian churchgoer.

The services are full of repetitions: "Lord have mercy, Lord
have mercy, Lord have mercy . . .", "Holy God, Holy and
Strong, Holy Immortal have mercy on us", repeated many
times over; and the full list of familiar repetitions would be
very long indeed. I used to think this excessive and I suppose
the services could do with some trimming, but it would be a sad
day if ever some rational and antiseptic liturgical reformer were
allowed to cut the repetitions right out. They set your heart and
mind in a groove of collective contemplation as nothing else
could do. In Orthodox services you are not supposed to maintain that intense conscious concentration that is the aim of our
shorter western services, both Protestant and Catholic. At cer-

tain moments the action demands concentration and you cross yourself, kneel or prostrate yourself or perhaps just obey the deacon's injunction to "Stand well", but there are periods when you can relax and just allow the other people to carry you along, while your heart and mind stay to all appearances still and quiet.

I have long known the Liturgy of St. John Chrysostom, namely the Orthodox service of Holy Communion, fairly well, but until this last visit I hardly knew Orthodox Evensong. What a mistake I had made! One evening I found myself just before the time for Evensong near the church in the Obydensky Pereulok, which, as said above, is frequented by some of the intelligentsia. As it was a little early, I sat down on a bench by the entrance. A woman came up to me and said, "Let us all subscribe for a common candle," so I gave her a few kopeks without being sure what the candle was for. Then an old woman came and sat beside me, very flustered. She had just seen some young men sitting stone sober, when a violent quarrel broke out and one of them struck another as hard as he could with a wine bottle over the nose. She had been too frightened to wait and see what happened. "What is the world coming to?" "But *babushka*, there have always been fights." She turned and looked at me almost fiercely and said, "Do you think so? Yes, there were drunken fights, and anyone can understand that. But now people do these things when they are sober." The service began. I meant to stay for half an hour, but the longer I stayed the harder it became to tear myself away. So I stayed to the end, two and a half hours later. The congregation arrived by degrees and must have numbered two to three hundred at their maximum. Most of them were working-class women, but among them there was a sprinkling of people who looked like Oxbridge professors, an intellectual young man whom I had seen before, and some very young and very pretty girls who knelt and seemed to be completely absorbed in their prayers. I think it was the feeling of peace that held me. All those repetitions impose their rhythm and seem to slow Moscow down to a speed at which one can live. As it got dark the congregation became a little thinner and we seemed to be a large family hemmed in by a circle of light in a sea of darkness, at peace with ourselves and with everyone. I remember something of the same feeling from my childhood in the west country, before electricity and other modern conveniences came to our remote, storm-swept hilltop. Sometimes on winter evenings by firelight and lamplight the family would be gathered, each aware of the others and each concentrated on what he was doing.

Orthodox worship is open-eyed, collective and physical. You do not kneel, shut your eyes and cover your face with your hands. For most of the time you are standing open-eyed and thoroughly aware of the sights as well as the sounds that surround you. You look at the icons but you look through them, for Orthodox holy pictures are only holy by reason of their transparency. They are symbols through which you see another world or, as I prefer to say, you see through them to the reality which is the ground of this world's being. This open-eyed worship is less individual than most of our western worship. You see the people around you and are aware of them in the way that one is aware of other people at a silent monastic meal, when no word is spoken but every need is anticipated and the table companions serve each other without impairing the interior silence.

Orthodox worship is tactual, as well as visual. The Russians are physically affectionate and men kiss each other lovingly without any homosexual overtones. And women will sometimes show physical affection to a man, without implying any sexual familiarity, in a way that a westerner can easily misunderstand. This physical affection is carried into church. All Christians want to kneel down and kiss the hem of Jesus's garment. The Russians do it, every time they go into church, by bowing, crossing themselves and kissing some of the icons lovingly, or, nowadays more likely, by kissing the glass that covers the icons. They seem just as happy to kiss the glass; it brings them just as near to Christ and his saints. When Russians cross themselves, they do not seem to be drawing imaginary lines in the air, but making a mark on forehead, breast, shoulders; one thinks of the nails.

All the senses have their share in worship, for the spiritual is not opposed to the bodily. Salvation is not a displacing of the material by the spiritual but rather a transfiguration of body and soul. That is why the Transfiguration is such a great feast in the eastern Church. St. Gregory Palamas, one of the greatest eastern Orthodox teachers, who was Archbisop of Salonica in the fourteenth century, taught explicitly that the body shares in the bliss of transfiguration. So Orthodox worship speaks to the whole man with his five senses as well as his mind and heart, through words, things to be seen, things to be touched, incense and music.

The icons are less realistic than much western religious painting because they are symbols of something else and they must never be mistaken for that which they symbolise. The strictness with which the traditional rules for icon painting are kept differs with times and places, but an icon is always unmistakably an icon. Likewise, Orthodox music has its own style, though the chants differ greatly from country to country. There is never an organ or any other accompaniment, and the older tradition is a strict chanting in unison, but this has been overlaid with polyphonic composer's music since the end of the eighteenth century so that people now find it hard to accept the unadorned traditional chants. Indeed, there seems to be some doubt about just how the old chants should be sung. Russia has had no Solesmes to restore her ancient music and teach her how to use it. None the less feeling runs high. The purists tell one that the sugary music one hears in most churches represents the taste of the Russian merchants of the last century. I was given some rare records of Russian church music by the Moscow Patriarchate and I showed them to some friends. Their verdict was that the monks at Zagorsk sang beautifully and in the proper Orthodox style, but that the well-known choir of the church on the Bolshaya Ordynka was a disgrace; and the collaboration of famous opera singers, such as Kozlovsky, made it worse. Technically their singing was good but it was theatrical and destroyed the spirit of prayer. What did I think? I had to say that our experience in the west was different. You may want to scrap Stainer and Stanford and even Schubert's *Ave Maria* and want to substitute Gregorian or Anglican chanting or, for that matter, Scottish metrical psalms, but you cannot want to abolish Bach and Byrd and Palestrina. Then I told them about Donald Swann and Sydney Carter's church music. That surprised them and they asked eagerly for news about experiments in the use of modern styles of music in church. And what about modern church architecture?

There are generally two choirs in a Russian church. One of them stands on the right and may aim at a professional standard, though, so far as I can discover, its members are generally devoted amateurs. The other choir stands on the left and consists merely of keen members of the congregation. Even the right choir often consists mainly of the elderly, for it is only those who are retired and whose families are grown up, who can afford the time. I calculated that in one church I know a regular and conscientious member of the choir would have to spend about thirty-five hours a week in church, and more at the great festivals. Those who do this are the simple people who have grown with the services all their lives, know them and love them. The left choir can be rough and unpolished but, when they get going, they sing with a fervour to move mountains.

Sometimes one is invited to stand behind the iconostasis, and on one occasion I was in a position from which I could see nothing outside the sanctuary. That day there was a lot of *vechnaya pamyat*, eternal memory for the dead, sung by the left choir. How some of those little tunes haunt one! They sang simply and not very well, but in such a manner that one forgot everything else. There was no proper deacon and the deacon's part was sung by a woman. She stumbled over some of the Old Slavonic in the Epistle, but the message came across, clear and strong.

In another church I was greatly helped by the *Psalomshchik* (psalm man). I had not realised what a skilled technician a good *Psalomshchik* is. He, or in some churches the *Chtets* (reader), is responsible for seeing that a very complicated course of services throughout the year runs smoothly, and with beauty and reverence. His is a whole-time job, ranking lower than that of a deacon. This *Psalomshchik* was a good man whose ambition was to be a priest, but he had not been able to get the necessary education. He helped me to find the place in the service books by pointing with his finger, and at last I understood what the Orthodox do to the Magnificat. They do sing it all through, but a little hymn to the Blessed Virgin comes as a refrain between each verse, which got me hopelessly mixed.

One day there was a christening. Baptism in the Orthodox Church is by total immersion. When my Orthodox nephews and nieces were christened in London it took two or three hours. I asked the Archimandrite Nicholas Gibbs, a Russified Yorkshireman who had been tutor to the Tsarevich, whether the service could be shortened but he said, "No. If it is shortened, it isn't a proper christening." The Anglican godparents were perplexed when they were told to blow and spit on the devil. "No," said the Archimandrite, "not like that, don't spit on the baby. Spit on the devil. Over there," and he pointed crossly to the north, which is the devil's direction. This time it only took twenty minutes. The candidate was a tearful little girl of two and a half, who could not make out what was going on, and why she was being given such a funny bath in a strange place, but she cheered up when they anointed her legs and hands and breast, explaining that it was being done so that she could "Go better". The mother is not allowed to be present at a Russian christening, so the little girl was held by her grandmother, who made the responses, and knew well where to locate the devil. When she was asked whether she had renounced Satan, she had to answer in Old Slavonic *Otrekokhsya*, and she said this word with unforgettable force.

One day a priest asked me point-blank, "What is your attitude to the Orthodox Church?" "I am completely happy to be an Anglican. That is where God has put me, but if I lived in an Orthodox country I would be Orthodox. There are many apparent differences between our churches but at the deepest level there is no difference in faith. On the whole I think, myself, that the eastern Church has kept the proportions of the

Christian faith better than any of our western Churches, but
the difference is not fundamental." "Then you can make your
communion with us." "That would be the greatest joy to me, a
joy that I would not have dared to ask." "First you must make
your confession. Do you have any objection?" "I know your
rule about that and I will gladly obey all your discipline."

I spent the next two or three days trying to remember my
sins and to think out how to say them in Russian. When it was
too late, I was told that I should have also have been sparing
in food and drink, but I don't see how I could have refused
Russian hospitality. The night before you make your communion you are supposed to go to Evensong, which of course
takes two or three hours. I could have sat for part of the time
but I thought I had better behave like a proper Russian and
stand. So I stood with the choir, who all knew I was to make
my communion, and gave me a very warm welcome. One of
them thanked me afterwards, as if it was not I who was the
debtor. The Russian Christians value every sign that brothers
and sisters in other lands stand beside them.

Then I went back to the priest's flat to make my confession,
but first he plied me with tea, home-made cakes and home-
made jam on a scale that seemed to contradict what he said
about the desirability of having only a light meal. The confession involved a pretty searching examination, and was as
terrifying as it ought to be. One kneels before the icon of Christ
and is reminded that his eye sees all. The priest then addresses
one. "Behold, my child, Christ stands here invisibly to receive
thy confession. Be not ashamed, nor afraid, and conceal nothing from me—but without hesitation tell me what thou hast
done, and receive absolution from Jesus Christ. Behold his picture before us! I am only a witness, and certify before him all
that thou tellest me. If therefore thou concealest anything from
me thou wilt be doubly sinful." As I recounted my sins, he
repeated "Lord forgive!" and at the end, when he pronounced
God's absolution, he put a veil over my head and placed his
hands on it. I felt my sins were covered and God would look on
them no more, even if I could not expect or want to forget them.

The priest then came for me in a taxi at ten to eight the next morning and made me stand beside him in the sanctuary for the elaborate and beautiful service of preparation which precedes the liturgy. One receives communion in both kinds out of a spoon and standing up. After that one is given a dry little loaf called the *prosforka* to eat with a cup of wine mixed with water. I found it rather hard to get down and had not realised that I was supposed to eat it quite so quickly. It is not consecrated, so I thought it would not matter when a crumb was dropped, but an old lady picked it up with a horrified look and ate it. The rule that women must not go inside the sanctuary seems to be going out fast. All my family, both living and dead, were mentioned both at the liturgy and at a special little service or *moleben* afterwards, and I was given another *prosforka* to keep as a memento.

After my communion I was congratulated according to custom and given some marvellous prayers of thanksgiving in Slavonic to read to myself at a desk. Then there were various services for the dead with the usual cakes and corpses and some abandoned expressions of grief. After that and a good deal more, it was time for my *moleben*. One of the left choir and I bowed our heads low to support the Gospel while it was read. Once again Orthodoxy was shown as the most tactile of all forms of Christianity.

The weekday liturgy is considerably shorter than the Sunday liturgy but even so it was after eleven before it was over and I was glad of a sofa to sit on, a glass of tea to drink, and a slice of dry bread to munch. There is a Russian word *podvig*, meaning any feat involving physical, mental or spiritual endurance, and to make one's communion is considered to be in its way a *podvig*. Later the priest's family asked about communion in the Church of England and I explained our customs. They are always surprised that we kneel to receive. "And how often does a believer communicate?" "Everyone makes his own rule, but nowadays it is very usual for a firm believer to make his communion every week, as in the early Church." There were gasps of surprise. "And there are those who make a daily communion."

I do not think I have ever said anything that caused so much astonishment.

Once or twice I felt a wave of joy passing through the church, as a beloved priest appeared. Both priests and people are extraordinarily observant about any new person who comes in to their church. He may be a brother, an inquirer, a government spy, a disturber of the peace, a mere gaper, or a stranger. They size him or her up by the way he or she "stands" and they seem to have a sixth sense about who is genuine. The question of how you "stand" is very important and has all sorts of overtones. A priest who wants to know what you think of his congregation will ask eagerly, "How do our believers stand?"

CHAPTER XII

The Czech Events

On my first visit to Russia, in 1934, my travelling companion kept annoying me by retorting that it was no more striking than Prague, whenever I exclaimed at the strangeness of the Kremlin and the Red Square. I could not answer, because I had never been to Prague, and it was not till 1961 that I began to know that sad, beautiful city. By that time reality had caught up with Kafka's dream world of a generation earlier, and the Hradčin had, it seemed, become Kafka's Castle. But the streets from which he looked up at that symbolic building still kept their charm and were little changed since Kafka's time. Some of them, indeed, looked much as they did in Mozart's day, with their little shops nestling between mediaeval towers and baroque palaces. It was impossible, however, to forget the gigantic statue of Stalin, another symbol equally dominating the city but from another hill. On my next visit, in 1964, this statue had gone. Even under Novotny some things did change.

In Moscow in the 1950s one saw some men's clothing with an unmistakably western cut and smarter than was then usual. On inquiry one generally found that these came from Czecho-slovakia, and in the 1960s *avant-garde* plays in Moscow were sometimes adaptations from the Czech. If the Russians had imposed their form of government on Czechoslovakia, the Czechs had in return some small influence on their Soviet rulers.

If one had been parachuted into Prague about 1960, without knowing where one was, one would have seen at once that one was somewhere between Moscow and Vienna, but one would not have known how much nearer it was to Vienna. The street scenes had a mitigated drabness and the young behaved in a relatively free and easy way that would not have been tolerated

in Moscow until three or four years later. I was visiting Prague
as a delegate to the international Christian Peace Conference, a
movement organised by the Churches behind the iron curtain.
At first this was regarded with suspicion by the Christians from
the west and the third world but eventually many of us decided
that there were substantial advantages in participating in this
movement, provided that we went to the meetings with long
spoons. I was to visit Prague again in 1964 and 1968 in connection with this movement. It soon became clear that labyrinthine
inefficiency could be taken for granted. Hapsburg *schlamperei*
was multiplied by Communism. One joined a fairly short queue
to register for the conference but nothing was ready, nothing
seemed organised. The particulars of those attending seemed to
be jotted down haphazardly, so that nothing could be found
quickly. There were long whispered conversations in Czech
before the simplest things could be decided. Several queues for
different purposes criss-crossed each other and got hopelessly
mixed up. After several hours one emerged with a headache but
supplied with meal coupons and the address of an hotel. At the
sessions bad translation, bad wiring of loud-speakers and ear-
phones, and a murderous echo made it almost impossible to
follow what was happening, unless one was fluent in both
Czech and German, which were the dominant languages. The
Czechs had given the Austrian Empire many hidebound petty
officials. The type persisted and adapted itself to Communism
with dreadful facility. It was not surprising to learn that, if this
was the standard of efficiency, the Czech economy was slowly
grinding towards a halt, or that the economic decline eventually forced the reforms that led to the fall of Novotny and
then to the series of happenings, which in Moscow are euphemis-
tically called the Czech Events.

The public sessions of our conference, and of the subsequent
similar conferences which I attended, were mostly a waste of
time, but in private the atmosphere was friendly and relaxed.
Some lasting friendships were made, and one picked up some
odd scraps of knowledge. One day at lunch I sat between the
Grand Mufti of Tashkent and the Grand Mufti of Ufa, who

told me that a new and greatly improved translation of the Koran into Russian was being made. To me they spoke not very good Russian and to each other they spoke a mixture of Russian and their respective variants of Turki. At this conference we were all called "brother", the Patriarch of Antioch being "brother Patriarch".

An Irish friend, who knew Russian but no Czech, observed that, if you know Russian, Czech sounds as if you could understand it, but it all turns out to be jabberwocky. Occasionally a completely intelligible sentence comes through and I saw that if I worked hard for a month or two I could get by in Czech fairly well, though I should always speak it with an atrocious Russian accent. Moreover, Russian can be a misleading guide to Czech. Instead of "Beware" one reads "Shame!" and in a church I read in stained glass "God is Petting. I John iv. 16". All Slavs think they talk Russian but sometimes this is an illusion. One lady said, "Oh, yes. Of course I speak Russian." But she then showed that she thought it was the same as Czech, which it isn't.

At that time one could get good and very expensive glass at Moser's on the Prikop, in German the Graben, and just occasionally some good cheap wine glasses. And the Slovak peasant shop on the Wenceslas Square had some very nice limewood spoons, etc., but, if you wanted to get something worth having, and to get it at a reasonable price, you generally had to go to the Tuzex shops, where you pay in foreign exchange, as in the Beryozka shops in Moscow. My Muscovite instinct was to go to the head of the queue, but in Prague even foreigners had to take their turn. It took two hours to buy a bottle of Slivovits and during that time I learned a good deal about Czech commercial customs. In efficiency it was about half-way between the Gum in Moscow and Marks and Spencers in Britain.

In the streets in 1964 there were a few very pretty well-dressed girls and it would not have been difficult to make a satisfactory pick-up. The fashion magazines looked a bit above the standard of a rather dim western country, and there were advertisements that looked as if the advertisers wanted to sell.

I remember one for umbrellas with a picture of a boy and girl caught in the rain and brought together by the shelter of an umbrella—and you wouldn't see that in Moscow. A colleague, however, summed up his impressions of the Prague streets by saying, "Eastern Europe needs a lot more bras and belts."

On my second visit to Prague, in 1964, I began to hear of neo-Marxists and dialogues between Christians and Marxists. At first I was very suspicious of these stories, but over the past five years I have gradually modified my opinion. I still suspect that some of those engaged in these conversations on both sides are unrepresentative, but there is no doubt that in Czecho-slovakia open-minded Marxists and open-minded Christians do exist, that some of them are people who matter and that they have been meeting each other. Eventually this could be important.

The Czech lands of Bohemia and Moravia are perhaps the least religious region in the Soviet bloc. Slovakia is another matter. My reading of history is that after Hus the Czechs were trying to find their own *via media* in religion but this was even-tually crushed by the Counter-Reformation followed by the Thirty Years War, after which the Czechs were under German domination. This forced on them "the German religion" of Counter-Reformation Catholicism to which the only possible alternative had become German Protestantism. It was a choice between two shoes, both of which pinched, and in consequence religion suffered. yet there is some real faith, both Catholic and Protestant in Bohemia and Moravia. One day in 1964 I went to see the *Jesulátko*, the Infant of Prague, that famous Spanish statue of the infant Jesus brought here by a Spanish noblewoman in Renaissance times. It was more beautiful and more impressive than I expected. The tiny, pale face of the Creator of the world is set in silver swirls of Austrian rococo and loving hands had dressed him in his best clothes. Quiet groups sat in the church, praying or gossiping in whispers, but the whole scene was pervaded by prayer. The seats face the high altar but all glances go sideways to the *Jesulátko*. It was summer and warm but nearly four years later, when I went back to this church at the beginning of April, it was freezing cold and I learnt that one of the ways in which religion was discouraged was to turn the heating off.

Between the sessions of the conference in 1964 my Irish friend and I went sight-seeing. I had a commission from another friend to get a reproduction of a picture in the National Gallery of Czechoslovakia, which must have been one of Europe's great galleries before the Hapsburgs moved most of the good things to Vienna. Now, however, no-one knew where it was, but all proffered confident advice. It was as if you asked the way in London and were told "The National Gallery? That's in Bloomsbury." "No, it's the Tate Gallery." "Yes, go to Manchester Square." "No, to South Kensington." "You can't miss it. Just ask for the Tower of London." "Or Buckingham Palace." By a wonder we found the right place, the Sternberg Palace in the Hradčin. There we saw a crowd going into St. George's Church, just beyond the great Cathedral. So we followed them in and got involved in a mediaeval mystery play about St. George. Not understanding Czech, we came out and sheltered from a thunderstorm in another church porch. As the storm was long, we had a long conversation in German with rather a sad elderly gentleman, who complained mournfully about the régime. Afterwards my friend said, "My Anglo-Irish neighbours have been talking exactly like that for forty years. So what is one to think?" In the evening we dined at a little bistro I had had my eye on for two days. It was rather above the European average for such places and it was not expensive; the air was filled with sounds of the Beatles.

My third visit was for a week at the beginning of April 1968, in the days of the Prague spring when the sparkling sun-filled air seemed to answer to the nation's mood. The first impression, on a fine and warm Saturday evening, was of much more relaxation than four years before. People did not care whether they were noticed. So they dressed as they pleased. Many of the boys and girls could have passed for natives in the King's Road, but others could not. In a tram I met an elderly couple who were coming to Britain in a few weeks to visit their son, daughter-in-law and grandson, who had defected three years ago. They had no inhibition against talking about this to a stranger. Then I saw an animated group looking around them with obvious interest. So I went nearer and found that they were Russians.

Walking down the street I met a Czech friend, who said he had only just received his copy of *Frontier*, the quarterly magazine that I edit. I was glad both that the Czech censors read *Frontier* and that they let it through. They must have been reading it just at the time when they recommended their own abolition. I had been criticised for publishing in that issue some criticism of the leadership of the Prague peace movement on the ground that it was sometimes used by the atheist régimes. So I gave him a sharp look and asked him whether he had found anything to criticise in this issue. "Not at all," he replied, with the ghost of a smile.

I spent most of my evenings and some of my afternoons with Czech intellectuals, who were eager to compare their experience of Communism in their country with my experience of Russia.

One rather *square* but intelligent young man said, "It is very hard to get a flat. I have been engaged for two or three years but cannot get married because I have nowhere to live. However, my future brother-in-law is going to Moscow later this year. So I hope to have his flat while he is away and to get one myself when he comes back." He said, "Everything will change now, but I do not know how. This upheaval is a genuine renewal from inside the Communist Party, and not the result of pressure from outside the Party." He worked in one of the state trading organisations and thought that artisans such as cobblers and barbers, would now be given their head, but that private shops would not be allowed. "And agriculture?" "There will be no change there." But he grinned slyly, when I told him of the difficulties of the Soviet collective farms.

Another friend said, "It is much too simple to say that the changes here are an internal renewal of the Communist Party. There was no poverty, as poverty goes, but the whole nation had lost its morale and no-one bothered to work more than he had to." "No-one knows what will happen about the Party's monopoly of power, but that is not the important thing. The most important thing is to get rid of objectionable people such as the spies who control a block of flats, or the corresponding people in the hierarchy of a workshop or here in the Writers' Union," where we were meeting. "Those who have committed crimes must all be tried, but after that they can be pardoned. There is no need for vengeance, but the truth must be established. Sometimes the persecutor is still living in the flat of his victim and the libraries of writers have been taken by other people. Such things cannot be put right without a trial." Then he left me for a few minutes to speak to the secretary of the Writers' Union, explaining afterwards, "We must get rid of the Stalinists here, too. There is a woman here who is known to be an informer. She must be got rid of, but it must be done fairly and quietly." After this a young poet came up. He knew no foreign language, because he had spent six years in a concentration camp at the time when he should have been studying. He had just been at a meeting of people who had been condemned for political crimes. "We have this evening formed our own association. It is called the K 231 association after the article of the criminal code under which we were sentenced." And under that name it became a principal object of Soviet hostility. This was a quiet evening at the writers' club. Few people were there and no-one raised his voice or gesticulated. Yet one could feel a thrill in the air.

Another writer was less resilient. He feared that the revolution would get stuck quarter-way. He agreed that already things were much less bad, but as he spoke, his face looked haunted. In Communist countries I have seen a strangely similar look on the faces of those who have done terrible things and of those who have suffered terrible things. For this particular man Prague was above all a city of unhappy memories. When he was eighteen Hitler came in. He was studying at the Charles University. Then one day he found it shut and German soldiers at the door. After the war he went back to his studies, but was expelled after the Communist take-over in 1948. "I

10

hardly know what the truth is after all the terrible things I have seen. But the young are wonderful. They have courage and honesty."

In central Europe I always call educated men "Dr. So-and-So", but generally the Czechs corrected me, saying, "I am not a doctor. For political reasons I was not allowed to finish my studies." A young man said, "My father fell foul of the authorities. So they punished me, too, by expelling me from the university. After that I worked as a labourer for six years. So I know our workers. They are supposed to be apathetic but they are not. They see quite clearly that the cause of the intellectuals is their cause, too. I know Russian but I have an emotional stop about speaking it. Yet I should like to know the Russians, to understand their youth. Do you think I could get permission to live in a Russian village for six months?"

An intelligent but shy girl said, "I have never really got to know the thoughts of my own generation, because my father was in political trouble and people shunned me. They didn't allow me to go to the university."

Once one of the party arrived late and out of breath. He had been to a meeting to found an association of those who had been unjustly expelled from university. For people with an academic career it was important to have the degrees they had earned. Often students who denounced their comrades are now professors. Generally such people are not up to their jobs. Now they must be edged out and better people, who will often be political victims, must take their place.

One evening I asked about Marxism but everyone present said he knew no Marxists. "There are Party members, but they simply repeat phrases. None of them think in a Marxist way." "The Party has killed Marxism." "Or the -ism has killed Marx." Thinking Marxists had either been expelled from the Party and ceased to be Marxists in any effective sense, or else they were working themselves out of Marxism. "At least that is what they are really doing but some of them suppose that they are helping to re-make Marxism." I asked about the neo-Marxist, Machovec, who has a certain reputation in the West.

They all laughed. "He is a bigot. He was a Catholic bigot. Then he became a Marxist bigot and for all we know he may now be a neo-Marxist bigot. In any case he remains a man of very narrow understanding."

Yet one should not underestimate the agony of believing Party members. And such people do exist. One said, "I know that the Party has sunk very low in popularity. I know that if there had been no *putsch* in 1948 the Party would still be large and influential, like the French and Italian Parties." Yet he maintained that the *putsch* was necessary to forestall a counter-stroke. Another Party member of twenty-five years' standing, and the son of a Party member, was pleased but bewildered by what was happening. He admitted that so far Communism had always meant tyranny and hoped that there could now be a genuinely free and democratic socialism, but he said the young were sceptical about this and he seemed to be pretty shaky himself. His instinct was to think that, once you gave up Marxism, socialism goes; but his thoughts on this matter did not seem properly worked out. I said there could be public ownership of the principal means of production and distribution without Marxist ideology. This puzzled him. He seemed to think it was theoretically possible, but the idea was new to him and obviously his instinct was to feel that socialism will be eroded, unless there is an ideology to support it. There is, after all, a similar argument about whether in the long run you can have Christian morality without Christ. When I met this man, he was reading Deutscher and other western Marxist writers, who had been inaccessible to him for twenty years, and I had the impression that he was working himself out of Marxism, but since then the Party's generally patriotic behaviour in the face of the Russian invasion has regained much of Communism's lost popularity. The effect of this on ideological evolution is not yet discernible.

During these days when I was in Prague, the Central Committee of the Communist Party was having its crucial meeting in the Hradčin, when the Stalinists were routed. I cannot speak from first-hand knowledge of what happened afterwards, but at that moment there seemed to be no question of the Party giving up its political monopoly. The idea was to have freedom in a Communist framework. It was a bit like Frederick the Great's "My people and I get on very well. They say what they like and I do what I like." Few people seemed to see that sooner or later the people would want one thing very badly and the Party would want another, and that then the Party would have to choose between taking freedom away or giving up its monopoly of power.

On 1st April, President Johnson announced the withdrawal of his presidential candidacy and his offer of peace negotiations in Vietnam. This was bound to affect our World Christian Peace Conference and I noted in my diary: "At any rate we shall be spared some of the anti-American tirades." But I was wrong. The Czechoslovakian news agency published a weakened version of Johnson's change of policy; the Russian Church delegation were manifestly taken aback by the news but soon they seemed to have received fresh instructions to secure a condemnation of Johnson's "hypocrisy" at any cost, and most of the other east European delegations followed them. This did not pay off. All the Africans and Asians whom I spoke to saw through the manœuvre and were disgusted. The climax came at the height of a heated debate on Vietnam. Some irenic and very sensible amendments put forward by the American delegates were voted down by the block votes of the east. And a South Vietnamese made a speech which conveyed, to my mind at least, that he wanted to humiliate America more than he wanted peace. Then one of the British delegates whispered to some of us that he had heard on his transistor that Hanoi had accepted negotiations with Johnson. My friend handed a note to the vice-chairman of the meeting, a fellow-traveller from the west. He looked embarrassed, twirled the paper, looked at it upside down, put it down, and then, after a very long interval, put it where the chairwoman could just see it, if she happened to look that way. The Russians continued to denounce Johnson's double-faced offer. Then the chairwoman saw the paper and read it to us. Some applauded and some looked the other way.

That evening I dined with Czech friends again. Every day I was becoming more hopeful. The Czechs and the Slovaks, too, though I saw less of them, seemed to be playing their hand with wisdom and much courage. There were some dangerous rocks ahead, but at that moment the dangers to come seemed nothing by comparison with the difficulties that were past. I thought that, if I were younger and more foot-loose, I would come to Czechoslovakia for six months, learn their language and share their experience. To see that light of dawn was an experience that only came once in a lifetime.

I reasoned, with many others, that the Kremlin had already missed the moment when an armed intervention might pay off, as it did in Hungary in 1956. But what would happen? "Socialism with a human face" in Czechoslovakia was bound to be contagious. Yet it threatened the vested interests of the Soviet ruling class.

Five and a half months later, on 21st August, I was travelling in the Russian provinces when the Soviet and satellite forces invaded Czechoslovakia. I first learnt what had happened from a taxi-driver. "Have you heard the news? The Czech government [*sic*] has invited the Warsaw Pact powers to send in troops. And our troops are already there." "That is bad, very bad." "Yes, it is very bad." But he did not mean what I meant. Subsequent conversation showed that he was indifferent to the moral aspect of occupying someone else's country. He was frightened of war. And that was all. "We ought to have annexed all those east European countries to the Soviet Union after the war. We could have done it then, couldn't we? And it would have saved all this trouble." "Yes, you could have done it, but that would have been imperialism." Speechless surprise. Such reactions proved typical of the uneducated classes.

It took two days before I was certain just what was happening. During this time I asked repeatedly whether there was any news and the answer came every time, "So far, nothing." At first I wondered if the reports I had heard were inaccurate, as in some respects they were, and if this answer meant that an ultimatum had been given to Prague, but the troops had not moved in. But no, all they meant was that the west had made no menacing counter-move. No-one I spoke to even pretended to believe the revised official story of an invitation from a group of members of the Czecho-Slovak Communist Party, members of the Central Committee and members of the government. When I exploded and said this would not deceive a child, the answer came cool and cynical, "Of course not." But there was always an ominous silence when I asked, "What kind of peace can there be after this?"

The Russian working classes are terrified that the policy of their government and of other governments will lead to war. But the despotism and cynicism of Soviet rulers for more than a generation has made the people almost indifferent to the moral conduct of their government. They are loyal, but what the government does is nothing to do with them. In that sense they are completely alienated from their rulers. They give a mental shrug to their shoulders and say, "If only there is no war." The attitude of the intelligentsia was very different. Some were shocked by the moral apathy of the working class, and said, "Is there no longer any sense of Russian honour?"

I was in Russia for a month after the invasion and I learnt what was happening, as the days went by, as a Russian learns it, by reading *Pravda*—particularly by reading between the lines—and by bush telegraph. I surfaced occasionally to see the embassies and the foreign journalists; and in any generalisations that follow I take their views into account. They filled in some very interesting details for me, but the general character of the events was quite clear without that.

One could see at once that security was being tightened up. My first night in Moscow they woke me twice, once by telephone and once by knocking at the door. This is an old trick of the Ogpu, designed to make sure that one is in one's room. And people became very careful what they said. Poker-faced Moscow gave no direct indication of her feelings at all. But on crucial days the Soviet papers were sold out early in the morning. Latterly the chief foreign papers have been on sale in the Intourist hotels, but now they ceased to arrive. This became known instantly throughout Moscow and it told us that foreign public opinion was solidly against what the Soviet Union had done. Even the foreign Communist papers failed to arrive. So we knew that the foreign Communist parties were not supporting the Soviet Union. This was confirmed when we read in *Pravda* a supporting resolution from the Communist Party of Uruguay; was that all that could be got by scraping the barrel? Even the flow of supporting messages from inside the Soviet Union seemed thin and rather jerky. The most popular foreign broadcasts in Russian were jammed and people said openly, "We none of us know what is happening now that the B.B.C. is jammed." Of course the Voice of America was jammed, too, and people began to discuss eagerly what alternative sources there were. "You can hear Belgrade in Russian." "No, now that is being jammed too." "You can hear Paris." "You can hear the Swedish broadcasts in Russian." "That is very interesting." And they would discuss the relative utility of the various services. "Paris doesn't give enough news." The Vatican Radio is fairly widely heard but does not always strike the right note with its parsonical voices and parsonical remarks; one of its speakers seems to have no teeth and I was given a vivid imitation of the Russian equivalent of "Thish ish she Vatican Radio." In general jamming is completely effective in the big cities and on the most widely-used wavelengths, but less so in smaller towns and quite ineffective in the countryside. Even people with *dachas* some distance from Moscow could hear through the jamming. It would hardly be feasible to jam every obnoxious wavelength continuously all over one-sixth of the land surface of the earth. And the B.B.C. broadcasts on some wavelengths that cannot be got on Soviet-made radios, but only on foreign sets; these wavelengths were not jammed. I heard afterwards that the price of Japanese transistors with these extra wavelengths went up by ten times in Moscow between 21st and 28th August.

After a bit the foreign Communist papers started arriving erratically. Copies of *L'Humanité* were snatched eagerly. When any paper did not come, one could sometimes guess how it had offended. The *Literaturnaya Gazeta* attacked Aragon and after that *L'Humanité* was unobtainable for two or three days and one could only guess what he had said, till the censor made a slip and let an issue of *L'Humanité* through with a reply by Aragon, which let the cat out of the bag. One day a copy of *Rude Pravo* from Prague arrived; it did not seem likely to comfort the Kremlin by what it said, but it was worth showing the Muscovites that *Rude Pravo* really was appearing again.

For the first two or three days you would have thought from the Soviet press that a deathly calm prevailed in Czechoslovakia, and the Soviet public were told very little; but soon *Pravda* and *Izvestiya* began to publish a full page of reporting from Czechoslovakia every day. This was very interesting reading. I quote from my diary for 31st August, ten days after the invasion. "The headlines and the opening sentences of the articles shout confidence but the subject-matter which follows shows that the situation is by no means under control and that the Soviet forces have no means of bringing it under control without using force on a scale that would be likely to cause a national uprising. I have just read an article saying that the morale of the Soviet troops is standing up well to a difficult task, but the fact that such a question is raised makes one wonder what the real answer is?" In church it was strange praying in every liturgy for the Soviet Army in the customary words that have come down from Byzantium. Many must have prayed specially for the army of occupation. I know I did. At one moment much play was made with a story of a Soviet tank crew who plunged over a precipice rather than run into a crowd of women and children. When I was told this, I said drily that I hoped there would be many Soviet soldiers who would prefer to lose their own lives rather than fire on the workers. The only answer was a sad little nod. On 1st September I was lucky enough to get a stray copy of *Die Neue Zürcher Zeitung*, and I wrote in my diary "*Pravda* gives me the impression that the Soviet difficulties are greater than the *Neue Zürcher Zeitung* seems to think. Both sources give roughly the same picture of the activity of the underground radio stations." I found later that the Czech and Slovak underground radio was fairly widely heard in the southern parts of the Soviet Union and, it seems, fairly widely understood; I understand that there was a good deal of Russian on these broadcasts. By the 5th September, a fortnight after the invasion, I was already speculating about whether some of the published reports were not deliberately intended to make the official policy look foolish. It was obvious that the Soviet leadership was divided and the only way the opposition could make their points was by letting through reports that asked to be read between the lines. The *Moskovsky Komsomolets*, which is designed for Moscow youth, had a story that the old Communists of Moravska Ostrava had passed a resolution declaring that they did not regard the Soviet Army as "occupiers", which is a rude word in the Soviet vocabulary. It seemed obvious that the message which Moscow youth would get was that many other people did regard the Soviet forces precisely as "occupiers".

Various means were used for drawing me on the invasion. It might be said with possibly genuine surprise, "Is it not hard that the Soviet troops should be greeted with such hostility in Czechoslovakia?" "Did you expect them to kiss your boots? You have seized someone else's land." Then the various Soviet arguments would be produced rather coldly and I would reply with heat. At the end the subject would be changed and I would realise that I had been drawn and that no-one else had committed himself. Reflecting that what I had said might go straight back to the K.G.B., I always said, "You started this conversation, not I. I would never start a subject like this, but if you start it I am bound to say what I think and feel." In those days I did not hear of many who made a thorough-going defence of Soviet actions, such as one heard continually in the bad old days of twenty or thirty years ago, but there was much half-hearted defence. No-one likes to believe that his country has committed a crime. In such a case one clutches at even a straw of justification. I waited for the Russians to start but if they did attempt to justify what they had done, I tore it to pieces; and the strange thing is that there was no fight in them. It reminded me of the conservative theologians of the Curia at the last session of the Vatican Council, when I was one of the

Anglican observers; they would produce their traditional arguments parrot-fashion but, when they were attacked by cleverer and more learned people with modern minds, they caved in at once.

However, as time went by, the mood changed perceptibly. Even at the beginning a certain heat came in when I was asked more than once, "How many of our soldiers are buried in Czechoslovakia?" To which I replied, "That only makes it worse. You are bringing shame on their memory." And after two or three weeks some Russians had already half convinced themselves that the invasion had forestalled a West German take-over. So far as the Kremlin's propaganda was concerned this particular justification was an afterthought. And it was absurd. But argument was useless. The Russians do not hate the Germans, but they are so frightened of them that they cannot think straight.

It is easy to mock, but the agony that lay behind these waverings was unmistakable. Even before "the Czech Events" most intellectuals were deeply disturbed by the way things were going. It was even possible to hear it said, if one may believe second-hand information, "The war years were a better time." This is manifestly not true, but I was horrified to find how bad things had become. The budget for internal espionage must be almost as large as it was under Stalin, though the penalties for being delated are now far less, as well they might be. The foreign journalists said things had suddenly become much worse in April after a warning speech by Brezhnev. It seems to have been at this point that the more dim-witted of Russia's rulers realised how serious the direction of events in Czechoslovakia was for them. If a Russian Dubček were to come to power almost all the present rulers plus, say, a hundred thousand of their closest supporters, would go out of office and many of them would risk trial on very serious charges, if the full enormities of Stalin's rule were unmasked. So it is essential for them to prevent the intelligentsia getting out of hand in the way they did in Czechoslovakia. "The Czech Events" have stirred the Russian intelligentsia to the depths, because every one of them feels "This is about me".

CHAPTER XIII

Rumanian Excursion

What happens in other countries of eastern Europe can help one to get perspective about the Soviet Union. In June 1968 during a critical period for the Soviet bloc I had the good fortune to spend a fortnight in Rumania. This was my first visit, but I was with friends who knew the country well; so, I was able to see things that I should otherwise have missed, and to check my impressions against their knowledge.

Landing at Constanza, our chartered aircraft taxied aimlessly along miles of concrete, apparently losing its way, while herds of sheep browsed on the grass beside the runways and friendly but tattered shepherds waved greetings. They wore stripy bundles of clothes and looked not unlike the Vlach shepherds I used to see in Greece many years ago. Vlach means Wallachian and therefore Rumanian, but their clothes were so worn that one could not quite see what they were meant to be. We landed; friendly people waved us on from one building to another and poker-faced girls sat behind desks doing nothing in particular. It looked like a long wait without either our passports or our luggage; but no.

Ten years earlier the customs people had been so suspicious that they held a priest's communion wafers to the light one by one to see if they concealed a code. This time the customs passed us through at once; we could have smuggled the crown jewels; and soon we were in a bus made in eastern Germany listening to sexy Latin music on the loudspeakers. Then two actresses came on with what one could tell was most improper backchat, though I could not understand a word. The bus went spinning along between wheat fields full of weeds, interspersed with rich vineyards and neat little one-storey cottages, freshly painted with nice gardens and roofs in good repair and garnished with T.V. aerials. On the whole it was a smiling and prosperous scene.

Everything was un-Slavonic, though very east European. With Slavs to the east, north and south of them the Rumanians neither look nor behave like Slavs. There has been inter-marriage and by the Black Sea coast one sees some swarthy Levantine types to remind one of the long Turkish domination, but the typical Rumanians are tall and bony with tapering faces and a reddish tint to their skin—"like Red Indians without their war paint" was the description of an artist friend. By contrast the Slavs are thick-set and inclined to have round faces with flat features. The gypsies are still much in evidence and look like the Victorian paintings of them; both they and the Rumanians have slender figures, whereas the Slavs are inclined to be dumpy.

I stick to the traditional English spelling "Rumania", but the country calls itself "Romania" to emphasise that its peoples are of Roman origin, though for a time Stalin made them call it "Romînia" as part of an attempt to make out that the Rumanians are not Latin but Slavs. Their language is a mixture, preserving more of its Latin base than either Italian or Spanish but with an admixture of many Slavonic words. The vocabulary is two parts Latin to one part Slavonic. If one knows Latin, Italian and Russian, one can often guess the meaning, provided one can tell whether a word is Latin or Slavonic in origin; but there are many surprises.

I was not prepared for the strength and originality of Rumania's national tradition. I knew that, for long one of the worst governed provinces of the Ottoman Empire, Rumania had then become one of the worst governed countries in Europe. I knew that at one time Bucharest was considered "the Paris of the Balkans", but what sort of Paris would one find in the Balkans? Ruritania was somewhere near, and how could one take a comic opera country seriously? True, I had been told that the Rumanian Orthodox Church led the Balkans in scholarship and had a more vigorous life than any other national church under Communist rule, but how far did that take one? Rumania had only emerged into full light of history at the end of the Byzantine period and she had fallen under the Turks before she had time to grow to her full strength. Lying between the spheres of a decadent Byzantine culture and an unripe Muscovite culture her own culture must surely be provincial. It was true that even under the Turks she had been able to stipulate that she would be ruled by Christian princes, but their rule was unusually corrupt. Much of this may have been true, but it was at best only half the truth. The cards were stacked against Rumania, but she had found her own devious solution to insoluble problems. She had, in spite of all, made her own beautiful and original variant of the Orthodox east European civilisation and this had been enriched by five generations of intimate contact with French culture. The Rumanians felt their national identity as passionately as anyone. In the long run, with their culture that was both Latin and eastern Orthodox, they might be better placed than anyone to mediate between the thought of eastern Europe and the west. And their land was naturally so rich and was now so well supplied with the "infra structure" of education and communications that they were posed for a rapid leap forward.

In June, Bucharest is a city of red roses flourishing luxuriantly, unpruned and ramping like creepers. The city is big enough for a capital but not overgrown like London or Paris, let alone *Boswash*. On one side it has a fringe of lovely lakes like Berlin, but as one approaches it across these lakes one comes to the monstrous building of the newspaper *Scînteia* (the Spark), which houses an enormous combination of printing, newspapers and other publishing. It was designed by a Russian architect in the worst Stalinist style, complete with towers like Moscow University and is a continual reminder of the Russian domination after the war. The Rumanians, I soon found, are very skilful in suggesting what they feel about the Russians, by the words they use, and the words they omit, as well as by slight pauses and inflections of the voice.

In Bucharest one felt at once that every contact was watched. Some people avoided foreigners altogether. Everyone seemed careful what he said, where he said it and to whom, though there was no lack of friendly casual conversation, if one asked the way in French or English in a tram. A few years before, I was told, Rumanians fled from all contact with westerners in the streets. Even in 1968 most of the foreign journalists and diplomatists said they were cut off from effective contact with Rumanians, but I was left wondering whether they did enough to get across the very real but not impassable barriers. Too few of them knew Rumanian, journalists seemed to rely too much on flying visits, not enough time was spent in the provinces, where contacts were much easier than in Bucharest, and not nearly enough patience, ingenuity and imagination were brought to the task of getting inside an unfamiliar situation. I hope this judgment is too hard, but I do not think it is. However, it takes two to conduct even a *dialogue des sourds* and the Rumanian authorities can hardly complain if excessive security results in foreigners underestimating Rumania. But even so there is much to observe even in Bucharest.

Women are worked very hard, doing ordinary jobs on top of housekeeping. A Rumanian said that the men still have "an oriental attitude" expecting their wives to do *all* the housework and shopping and looking after the children as well as their other work, but he thought this would change. The Turks have now gone nearly a hundred years. The girls were quite well dressed, though with skirts too long for Chelsea. They can get quite good lengths of material in Bucharest or over the border in Budapest and there are thousands of little dressmakers who make them up. The men's clothes were shoddy and lost their shape almost at once, except for the few who were able to buy their clothes in the west. But Bucharest is a city which is determined to be European, and they will find out a way.

Students, too, were very hard worked, there being intense competition to get into college and to keep one's place when one has got in, the burden of examinations being severe, and attendance at a heavy load of lectures being compulsory. If you miss more than a very few lectures, you are expelled. "That's the university," said a student recently down from there. "We call it the Bastille, because it looks grim. There's the hostel where I lived, and there's the opera where we went without tickets, just tipping the door keeper." The Rumanians make a joke of everything. So far the students only demonstrate under orders, perhaps against the American Embassy in connection with Vietnam. "It was great fun. We left the active demonstrating to the Asians and Africans who got very excited. We thought that was comic. So we kept our own energy for teasing the police. We did enjoy that." On another occasion when we lost our way, it was suggested that we should ask a policeman, but this was treated with derision. "They never know anything. We think that all kinds of police are funny." But there is one kind of policeman whom nobody thinks funny. During our visit there were large-scale riots at Belgrade University, and I wondered if the "Bastille", too, might be in danger, but the government seized this moment to announce sweeping changes in the examination system and other concessions to the students. No doubt this was what they meant to do anyway, but the timing was good. So far, most of this was a variant on what one finds in other Communist countries but I soon realised that there were other elements which put Rumania in a class by herself. And notably the position of the national Church was far stronger. To describe Rumania without the Church would be like leaving religion out in a description of Ireland or Poland. Churches were open everywhere and crowded; even historic churches that fill no present pastoral need are in the custody of the Orthodox Church and used for occasional services. Priests wear their robes openly in the streets. Monasteries flourish, seminaries are full and there is a steady output of theological journals. To be Rumanian is to be Orthodox. The large Catholic and Protestant minorities are mainly Hungarian or German. Even atheists go to the Easter service and an atheist intellectual, when asked why he did so, answered in a puzzled voice, "But I am a Rumanian."

During our visit the Patriarch Justinian, the head of the Rumanian Orthodox Church, was celebrating the twentieth anniversary of his enthronement. For the first ten years of his Patriarchate he was generally regarded in the west as a church

Quisling and I remember looking at him with great suspicion, when we met by chance on the aerodrome at Kiev in 1958. Soon after that the shrewdest and best informed observers began to bring back reports that we had misjudged both the man and the situation. Justinian had always been a man with strong sympathies for the left. At the end of the war when Gheorghiu Dej, the Communist leader, was on the run, he had been hidden in his church by the future Patriarch, who was at that time a parish priest. And there are grounds for thinking that other most important Communists were helped by him in this way at a time when to do so carried a very serious risk. So it was not surprising that, on a vacancy arising, Justinian was made Patriarch. He used his special relation with the Communist leaders to advance the interests of the Church, while loyally supporting the socialist policies in which he had long believed. The Church had gone through very hard times in common with other Rumanians under the particularly brutal Stalinist régime installed after the war, but as the worst of the tyranny passed, it became apparent that the Orthodox Church was in an unusually favourable situation. The Patriarchate standing on a hill beside the Parliament House seems to embody a still existing partnership between Church and State in the national life.

Outside Bucharest the atmosphere is more relaxed. We stayed first at Mamaia, an insipid resort newly constructed on the sands of the Black Sea coast near Constanza, the ancient Tomi where Ovid spent so many years of mournful, stout-hearted exile. The road to Constanza led past little one-storey cottages, each different and each with its little garden. One felt that the traditional life goes on here, however the government may change. On a Sunday there was little traffic and people wandered up and down the streets, as in Italy. Girls, however, do not go about singly or, if they do, they may get molested. Rumania's sexual life was passing through a crisis. Until a year before, abortions had been free on request but the birth rate then went down so much that the government felt obliged to issue a decree making abortions illegal, under heavy penalties which were enforced. And contraceptives were not available, it being hoped that the birth rate would go up. The problems that arose *dupa decretul* (after the decree) can be imagined. Some solved their difficulties by crossing the "Friendship Bridge" across the Danube into Bulgaria, where one can be fitted with the necessary appliances, but one bridge was not enough for all the traffic.

Constanza has a new section but the old city is a typical, fairly prosperous, old-style Balkan town, not unlike some places in Greece. A Russian friend said it was very like a Russian provincial town before the Revolution, the same houses and the same shops. The great sight was the archaeological museum, which is worth a long journey. There was some delicate Greek jewellery of the fourth century B.C. from the Greek cities of the Black Sea and some later things which were so well shown that they stay in one's mind while similar things elsewhere make no impression. But the masterpiece is a Neolithic statuette about five inches high of a seated man leaning forward, plunged deep in thought. It could pass for the work of a modern sculptor under the influence of Henry Moore but with a mind of his own. The Dobrudja, the area between the lower reaches of the Danube and the Black Sea is one of the oldest homes of man in Europe. As on Salisbury Plain, one sees barrows everywhere on the Dobrudja skyline. It is inhabited by people whose mixed race shows in their features. They are reputed to be the stubbornest drivers in Rumania, men who would rather have a collision than give way; we watched their altercations at crossroads with curiosity.

Back at our hotel in Mamaia we had a celebration of the Holy Communion on the landing at the top of the stairs. In Russia the mere idea of such a thing would give the authorities a fit. Here it was taken for granted; the maids tip-toed by very quietly or, more often, stood throughout quite still on the stairs praying.

Leaving Mamaia we crossed the Danube by ferry at Hirsova after an hour's wait. From here the road leads across the Baragan, a barren and ugly part of the great plain that stretches from Hungary to China. After the war the Baragan was notorious as a place of forced labour. We lunched at Focsani on the edge of the Carpathians in an Edwardian restaurant newly done up in the contemporary style. The Rumanians have some good architects and interior decorators. It was a good meal and it was worth waiting till half-past two for it. Focsani is still a cosy, old-fashioned Balkan town with low stucco houses, no two alike. From here we branched to the right into northern Moldavia. The roads were good and the traffic was light, but included a few ox-carts and ass-carts and many horse-carts. These carts were all made in the same way, differing only in length; they were just wooden boxes put on the cross piece of a very low, broad H and with wheels added, not unlike the Russian peasants' carts. They were far removed from the replicas of Constable's 'Hay Wain' which were common in England between the wars. So few Communist slogans were up in the towns and villages that one turned to look at them. Towards evening we arrived at the splendid modern Hotel Ceahlau at Piatra Neamt in the foothills of the Carpathians. This is the chief centre for the reception of foreign delegations in this show part of the country. So, the secret police were in evidence and one of their tasks was to make the hotel efficient; they did that well. We had an excellent, well-balanced dinner with a bottle of good local wine and a band who would have been a credit to any provincial restaurant anywhere.

The next day was Orthodox Ascension Day. The air was filled with church bells and after breakfast we went into a beautiful little church built by Stephen the Great of Moldavia in the fifteenth century. Outside there were coloured ceramics let into the walls but it was spoilt by new roofing with very ugly red tiles. The inside was pretty with seventeenth-century furnishings. The Rumanian churches are unmistakably Orthodox but they have a different style from the Greek or Russian churches. There are no pews but there are *stasidia*, on which one may lean, if not sit, as in Greek churches. We went into several churches and, in the town at least, this being a working day, the congregations were only moderate in size, but they included all sorts and conditions of men, and all ages.

Having heard so much of Rumanian misgovernment and poverty in the past, I was not prepared for the degree of prosperity that was evident, here and elsewhere. One knew that the average wage was still very low and that housing was very overcrowded. Yet the people were well grown and obviously well fed. There were some shoddy goods in the shops but the standard was high enough for Rumanians who visited Russia to be horrified by what they saw in nearby Odessa. "But there's nothing at all to buy." "And I was shocked when an Intourist girl insisted that conditions were very bad in western Germany, although someone who had been there told her she was wrong. I said nothing but I was ashamed that she was so shameless. I, too, live in a socialist country."

Later in the morning we went up the Bistrita river to Bicaz where there is a hydro-electric dam built by forced labour during the 'fifties. The mountain air was good, in spite of some factories; Rumanian factories let out dirtier smoke than any I have seen. From here we went through a spectacular gorge among mountains to the Red Lake in Transylvania. On one of the hills were a large red star and a cross standing side by side. The Red Lake is in a predominantly Hungarian district and all the notices were in both Magyar and Rumanian, very bad Rumanian we were told. It seems that even now the Hungarian local authority has not learnt Rumanian properly.

This being Ascension Day, no work was done in the villages, though in the towns people had to work as usual. Most of the country people, men and women, young and old, wore their national costume. On the way up we saw a crowd coming out of church and in the same village on the way down there was a *tomasha*. So we stopped off. So far as Rumania was concerned, it was "God is gone up with a merry noise and the Lord with the sound of the trumpet". A wooden platform had been set up and there were two swarthy gypsy musicians, a fiddler and a man with an instrument that looked like a 'cello but which he used more like a drum. They were perched higher up than the rest, and beside them sat a little girl of two or three with fair hair and blue eyes, dressed in her best clothes and watching everything solemnly. At first only one couple was dancing, but soon others joined in. You can't dance unless you pay the musicians, the boy paying most but the girl paying something. The steps, I was told, were Moldavian but to dance in couples is Transylvanian; the real Rumanian dances are round dances. They did not dance very well, but their costumes were marvellous, being made of linen, sometimes patterned and sometimes pleated, with little sheepskin jackets for men and women alike. Both skirts and jackets were embroidered, all of them with different patterns and mostly new. Each embroiderer lets her imagination go and embroiders whatever she likes, wherever she likes. There was no rule but everything fitted, naturalistic flowers, geometric patterns, crowded or with airy spaces between. And the houses were painted as freely and elaborately as the embroidery was made, both houses and jackets often being dated, 1965, 1949, 1967, and so on. Transylvanian influence was seen in the number of houses painted a very bright ultramarine in the Hungarian style, but often trimmed off with an ochre that made a good combination. One house had a most elaborate pattern painted on its front wall. An expert said, "A bit like Transylvanian peasant pottery with a touch of Turkish and a touch of Paisley."

We talked to the crowd. "Yes, we have all been to church. But who are you?" "English." "But you speak Rumanian. Can you speak English, too?" "Yes." "All of you?" "Yes." "My two daughters are learning French at school. Can you speak Magyar?" "No." "Can you speak Russian? "No, but he can," pointing at me. And I got a look that made me want to hide myself. They seemed happy and fairly prosperous people. We said, "The drought has been bad this year. Will not the harvest be bad and will not people suffer?" "Yes, but we shall help each other. Those who have will give to those who do not have." This was said simply and quietly, as a plain statement of custom. It reminded me of the better side of Russian peasant life.

We spent the next two days travelling about northern Moldavia and the Bukovina, visiting the famous painted monasteries.

While we were on the road, I gazed with rapt concentration at the peasants' houses. I had never seen anything like it. Four years earlier, I am told, they looked dismal, unpainted and with leaking roofs, but now they were in good repair and every Rumanian village must have been using more paint than a fair-sized Russian town. Most peasant art is uniform or even monotonous but here there was variety. Every house was different, being tailor-made to each family's wishes, but always within the limits of an established style. Some of them were little masterpieces.

There was no standard design of roof or roofing material. I saw tiles, sheet iron, felt, asbestos, zinc, thatch and, above all, wooden shingles; even the shingles have no standard size and shape; one sees a different pattern on every roof. Each house tries to have a porch or veranda with several arches which are sometimes combined in the most beautiful proportions, and each porch or veranda differed with varying numbers and shape of Moorish arches and round arches, or with simple utilitarian glazing. Some of the houses are made of stucco with patterns moulded on it, no two patterns being alike. Nearer the mountains wood is more used and one sees fretwork patterns, not unlike those on Russian peasant houses. There was a wide range of colours, with ochres and ultramarine predominating. Some houses were simple, others had elaborate patterns made not only by paint but by varied materials. Each house expressed an individual character, more like the clothes in the King's Road than anything one expects to see in the Communist countries. There are, of course, sluts and *squares* in Rumania and one can see which their houses are. I saw, also, some wretched hovels and I should like to be sure that all of them are inhabited by animals and not by people. But all in all the effect was extraordinarily beautiful.

I saw something similar wherever we went but the best was in the Bukovina and northern Moldavia. Here in the last twenty years traditional peasant architecture has been adapted to modern needs and, as a Rumanian put it, "there has been an explosion of colour". No doubt most of these houses are pretty primitive inside; the widespread use of wells with picturesque well-heads is one indication of that. Some houses were made of sun-dried brick not properly mortared, but most were well built and even the worst of them had their own individuality so that one felt, "This is someone's home." Some of the tiniest cottages were beautifully arranged. However, Rumanian bourgeois taste could be atrocious. In this part of the country the fields were well cultivated right up to the edges, there was no waste land, and favourable slopes of the hills had recently been planted with orchards. Many of the sheep remained unshorn in June but looked in good condition. The cattle were fat and well looking and there were some lively horses. Rather a scanty hay harvest was being got in, this being a year of drought. In the ravines caused by heavy rain thorn-breaks were set to let the water through but catch the earth and prevent erosion. A Russian friend remembered from childhood his father teaching him always to have this done on the family estate in central Russia, as soon the as rain began to make a gully.

The chief object of our journey was to see the famous painted monasteries of the fifteenth, sixteenth and seventeenth centuries. These are painted all over inside and out; the Rumanians had some process by which outside frescoes will last for centuries, at least on the leeward side, even in a hard continental climate. The churches are high and narrow with very projecting eaves to keep the snow and rain off. I found it took time to get accustomed to their proportions but they grew on one. The subjects depicted scarcely varied but the treatment differed. On the outside west wall there was always a Last Judgment with an elephant waiting to go into paradise and in another place there would be a gory siege of Constantinople at some time in the dark ages with the besiegers dressed anachronistically as Turks. In scenes of martyrdom of all periods the torturers and executioners were always Turks—and most of these frescoes were painted while Moldavia and Wallachia were under Turkish rule. I suspected that if similar painting were executed now, Russians would take the place of Turks.

I will describe only three of the monasteries we visited, but each had its special character. Our first stop was Agapia, a famous and flourishing convent with at present three hundred and twenty nuns and forty more at an older convent near by, which has become a daughter house. Founded in the seventeenth century as a monastery for men, Agapia later became a convent for women and a very fashionable one. Grand ladies from the families of the Rumanian boyars and later from the bourgeoisie could retire here, living in their own houses and keeping their own servants. So, in addition to the peaceful monastic courtyard with a pleasing seventeenth-century church in the middle, there is a sort of monastic village outside the walls. Agapia still keeps some of its upper class atmosphere. It has a high standard of education, and we were shown round by a sister with a degree in theology. Under regulations made a few years ago monks and nuns under a certain age must have a good theological education or leave the monasteries. In a way this is good, but it is not known how many men and women with a real vocation to monastic life have been forced to leave. Now the monks and nuns have to keep themselves by working on the land and other forms of employment. So, Rumanian religious houses are perforce taking more and more to the active life and thereby becoming more like western monasteries. But contemplation will always be at the heart of their life. At Agapia we saw nuns working in a large vegetable garden in the village and there was a dispensary in the grounds clearly marked with a red cross. The place had a good feel and those who know say that it is now the best convent in eastern Europe.

In some Orthodox monasteries the monks and nuns share a common pattern of life. In others each man or woman lives in his own way; these last are called "idiorhythmic", but in modern times the common life tends more and more to become the rule. Agapia, however, is idiorhythmic, which seems to fit its aristocratic character.

If Agapia is the leading convent, Neamt is one of the leading monasteries for men. It has always been a centre for learning and it is here that the great Russian monk, Paisy Velichkovsky, was a *Starets* (or elder) at the end of the eighteenth century. It was through Paisy and from Neamt that the authentic tradition of Orthodox spirituality practised through "the Jesus prayer" became so widespread in both Russia and the Balkans. No Paisy, no Father Zosima in *The Brothers Karamazov*, and no *Franny and Zooey*.

In layout and appearance Neamt is like many other of the older Rumanian monasteries. Imagine a large courtyard surrounded by plain, well-proportioned buildings, strongly built for defence. Then imagine a tall, long church with a raked tile roof and enormously projecting eaves in the centre of the courtyard. The church has a covered narthex (or porch) with open walls and its main part is divided into three, a western section for the main congregation, a middle section with the tombs of founders and benefactors and a winding staircase leading to a secret room for valuables, and lastly a chancel for the monks crowned with a high "Moldavian vault", that is to say a series of rising circles and squares imposed on a square and leading the eye to a painting of Christ Pantocrator at the summit. The gilded iconostasis (altar screen) is much as in other Orthodox churches, but in Rumania the icons are painted in a more western and naturalistic manner. It was the evening hour and swifts flew in and out, while we were shown round by an archimandrite with a face of calm recollection. At the end he and an Anglican priest led us in prayer simply and sincerely.

Suceava, the chief city of that part of the Bukovina which remains Rumanian, the rest having been taken by the Soviet Union, is a historic city with old churches in the regular Rumanian style but in the back streets there was peeling stucco and some Balkan stinks. In the restaurant everything external was calculated to impress but the lavatory was well down to pre-war Balkan standards, which is saying a lot, and the wine was watered. The shops offered shoddy goods at reasonable prices and there was a splendid open air market; even at five o'clock there was a good supply of fruit, vegetables, cheese, cream, eggs, cornflour and the like, all at reasonable prices. I was tempted by some wild strawberries but resisted the temptation, since I had no means of washing them.

A few days later we visited another type of convent at Tiganesti in another part of the country. A Rumanian who was with us knew this place from childhood and wanted to visit it because he specially loved one of the nuns. So, we turned down a side road and backed along a village cart-track till we came to a footbridge across a little river. Crossing the bridge, we came first to a little village green, a rough triangle of grass with a covered well in the centre and cottages overgrown with roses all round. This led almost at once to the convent which was another green, rectangular this time. It had just enough shape to make it clear what it was, but there was no continuous wall to make an enclosure. One wandered in and out through the gaps in the little one-storey houses, which stood around not looking very different from the better peasant cottages. There was a low tower in the middle of one side and a little old church standing as usual at the centre of the green. We went in and found Vespers in progress. At first there seemed to be only two nuns, one chanting the office and the other making the responses, but gradually one became aware of quite a number of nuns scattered about in various attitudes in corners of the church, some kneeling, some crouching, some prostrate, but all rapt in silence.

Not all, however, were in church. A good half were working at the looms where they weave church textiles and do embroidery. A foreman was in charge of this work; he said he would not like to do anything else. It was a bit like the workshop of some cousins of mine, who in a small Irish village weave textiles that are exported to half the world; there was the same easy-going intelligent mixture of hand work and machinery.

In this land you are never far from the Church, but the very universality of the national religion makes it hard to judge its effect. When no-one is against the Church, not even those who have no faith in her teaching, what does it mean to be for her? The Rumanians are not a race of plaster saints but who wants plaster saints? A foreign admirer calls them "the happiest sinners on earth". A Rumanian who described himself as "very religious" added, "But I only sleep with my wife about once in

six months. We both believe in freedom. We believe in life."
Inconsistent, you may say. But this was a good man and his
goodness was bound up with his religion. I cannot explain
human nature, I can only describe what I see.

From Northern Moldavia we went over the Carpathians to
Brasov, formerly Kronstadt, in Transylvania, losing our way
because the city of Onesti once called after Gheorghiu Dej, had
just reverted to its old name for devious political reasons, but
the new signposts were not yet up.

Transylvania was formerly part of the Austro-Hungarian
empire. So, we had gone from eastern to western Europe.
Brasov was pleasantly Germanic, like a small garrison town in
Austria, and the crowds in the streets were different from those in
Moldavia. It being the western churches' Whitsuntide and therefore a festival for the Hungarians, they dominated the scene. They
are often darker than the Rumanians and lack their ruddy skin,
but the best way to tell them apart is by their walk and expression. They stride along with more purpose and have a touch of
that permanent scowl, which marks their distant cousins, the
Turks. One can see how in the old days they made short work
of the poor Rumanians. However, a Rumanian who had
visited most of the socialist countries, said Budapest was his
favourite city. The Hungarians are always very polite; at first
they are frigid, too; but "once they accept you as a guest, all
the barriers are down". The Russians and Bulgarians were very
friendly and human but "the Czechs and Poles make us feel
we belong to an inferior race". Central Europeans assume without question that they are better than eastern Europeans, almost
like whites with coloured people.

In Transylvania the Rumanians are the majority, but there is
a very large Hungarian minority and a smaller German minority.
Brasov, however, was a German centre. The Hungarian villages
are pretty with their blue paint and their little crosses on the
rooftops. They are not so individual as the Rumanian villages
but they are more orderly.

In the German villages one sees signs of a solid peasant culture, *Hausfraus* were out with their children, but most of the life

was hidden behind long, elegantly curving walls connecting all
the houses in a street and masking the gardens between. The
original purpose of these walls was defence, but the Rumanians
think it is unfriendly to keep such a custom up nowadays. The
different nations in Transylvania get in each other's hair and
I suspect they take offence too easily. The German villages were
charming, and to my eye at least they did not seem to be
unfriendly.

The Hungarians are half Catholic and half Reformed and the
Germans are Lutherans. In Brasov all the Hungarians and
Germans seemed to be taking Whit Monday off and in the
morning the churches were full. The Reformed church looked
like a school but I followed some people in and found it was
indeed a church and that it was decorated with garlands and
branches of fir for Whitsun, much as I have seen in Russia; a
young man in mufti was preaching a sermon in Magyar to a
packed congregation of all ages and both sexes in a large oblong
building with the pulpit stuck inelegantly in one corner. The
German church was a fine fifteenth-century Gothic building
with Persian and Turkish prayer rugs hanging on the walls. In
the Orthodox churches one sees lovely old Rumanian carpets
on the floor, not on the walls. I walked down the old Germanic
streets with never a new building in sight and found myself in
the Rumanian quarter. A building with spiky Germanic spires
roused my curiosity. It turned out to be the principal Orthodox
church, but it was in the wrong style, being not a Greek cross,
but an oblong building with an iconostasis and stasidia; there
were icons on the walls arranged like stations of the cross, one of
them being a seventeenth-century icon that showed Christ surprisingly with wings. Farther on the inhabitants of some of the
apparently comfortable old houses had to fetch their water from
a well. In Transylvania levels and types of culture criss-cross in
an individual way.

On the way back from Brasov we stopped at Sinaia, a mountain resort, like Switzerland must have been before it was
spoilt. Here there was an enormous royal palace. Something
between Balmoral and the St. Pancras Hotel. Leading members

of the Party had recently taken over some of the smaller palaces
in the grounds and the mocking Rumanians were already asking when "our new royal family" would move into the main
palace. Below the palace was a seventeenth-century monastery
which the Patriarch uses as his summer residence. Outside it
could almost have been Turkish with its spreading arches and
latticed windows. Inside the shingled roofs of the courtyard
swelled to make room for little mansard windows. The small
church, standing as usual in the middle of the courtyard had
frescoes of the late seventeenth and early eighteenth centuries.
These were fresh and vigorous, like some Romanesque and
Ethiopian paintings, with none of the tightness and conven-
tionality of icons of this period from Greece or Russia.

From Sinaia we descended into typical Rumanian plain
country with fat ducks and geese waddling beside the road. As
we passed through the Ploiesti oil field the air was heavy with
oil. Ploiesti itself had been more or less destroyed by Anglo-
American bombing and had to be rebuilt. A good many cars
were parked by the new blocks of flats and by east European
standards the place seemed prosperous; but it was colourless. In
the suburbs, however, the usual Rumanian cottage life was
going on.

One difference between Rumania and the Soviet Union is
that in Russia the Communist Party did at one time have the
wholehearted support of a substantial minority, whereas in
Rumania there were only about a thousand Communists in the
whole country when the Red Army came in. Subsequently their
numbers were indeed swelled, but not by true believers. The
Stalinist régime installed by the Russians was particularly
brutal, and therefore a bad advertisement for Communism.
This is not to say that the Communists did nothing for
Rumania. The cost was fearful and the brutality unnecessary,
but they did impose discipline on an undisciplined people and
they brought Rumania into the modern world. However, Communism is only a shell round a core of national life that is now
reverting to type. In the old days a teeming soil did not prevent
the kind of poverty that is caused by misgovernment. So there is

no nostalgia for the former social system, if there is also no enthusiasm for the ideology that is supposed to support the new system. Now a milder government is putting the national interest first and could already afford to open its doors a little wider. All the skeletons cannot be taken out of the cupboard at once but with every year the memories of the brutality and oppression of the 'fifties become a little more remote. There is still a danger of regression, but this would hardly be a regression to Stalinism. An ugly brand of home-grown authoritarianism is a greater danger. Nationalism, a background of anti-Semitism and a tradition of bad government make a good breeding ground for neo-fascism.

But this is looking on the dark side. On the whole the omens are good. In Rumania land, people and resources are in balance. The country is fertile, there is oil, and other raw materials for industry, and the distances are not too great. So, development is easier than in Russia and infinitely easier than in India. But easy or not, the progress is great. The oil fields provide the base for a modern chemical industry and, when the vast steel plant at Galatz on the lower Danube is finished, Rumania will be well equipped for further advance in heavy industry. Foreign policy will be canny and non-committal. One should not underestimate the Rumanians' ability to get what they want without any heroics or striking of attitudes. The reeds of the Danube Delta bow to every wind but, when the storm has passed, they bob up where they were before.

Czechoslovakia is a western country. So, one must be cautious in applying Czech or Slovak experience to the Soviet Union. Rumania, however, is an eastern European country. Much of what happens in Rumania today or tomorrow could well happen in Russia the day after tomorrow.

CHAPTER XIV

Signs of the Times

In this last chapter I try to plot the position of the Soviet Union
on its erratic orbit, placing my fragmentary but first-hand
experience in its context of what is known about the present and
the past from many other sources. Russia may yet change
direction for reasons that may or may not be predictable, but
we ought to be able to say where she has come from and in
what direction she is now moving.

The greatness of Russian achievement is beyond question, but
one must still ask what is the source and quality of this greatness
and what the probable achievement of the last fifty years would
have been without the Revolution. There is no need for this inquiry to be offensive. If the Russians are quick to resent criticism,
they are also self-critical. If you hector them, they brazenly deny
obvious faults, but if you sit and talk quietly and they feel that
they have your basic sympathy, they will volunteer honest and
wounding criticism of themselves.

The Russians, like many peoples, are fascinated by their own
past; and the picture of Tsarism is by no means one of unre-
lieved darkness. Before the Revolution Russia was, indeed,
beset with problems, but she was also a country of rapid
development. The industrial revolution had begun with the
arrival of John Hughes from South Wales in the Donbas in
1872, a little more than a hundred years after the beginning of
the industrial revolution in England; Russia passed what
would now be called "the point of take off" about seventy years
ago. Before the Revolution her rate of economic growth was
rapid, and sixty years ago she was already being called the
New America. Count Witte's far-sighted policy of railway
building had extended the "infra-structure" of communica-

tions far beyond industry's immediate needs. Without that Stalin's Five Year Plans would not have been possible. In the nineteenth century Russian science had already reached the highest excellence. The Mendeleyev tables of atomic weights were the work of the father-in-law of the poet Blok. Non-Euclidean mathematics were invented by Lobashevsky at the beginning of the nineteenth century and carried further by his follower Aksyonov. Soil science was a Russian invention and still keeps some technical words of Russian origin, such as *podzol*. In technology Popov invented wireless telegraphy simultaneously with Marconi. Russian university education was in the first rank. Primary education had lagged behind, but in the last years of Tsarism even, it was developing very fast. The big estates were breaking up and the land was rapidly passing into the hands of the peasants. The co-operative movement was growing fast. Even in politics striking advances had already been exacted from a most unwilling Tsar. There was also a dark side which is much better known and was indeed very dark by nineteenth-century standards, but legitimate Russian pride is not confined to the past fifty years.

Before the Revolution Russia was already poised for advance and, whatever happened, she was sure to become at some point in the twentieth century an industrial power second only to the United States. Her resources of land and raw materials were immense and she had a population who were just reaching the point when they would be able to exploit their natural advantages. After the Revolution Russia's advance continued to be rapid, becoming at times very rapid indeed; but it also became jerky; there were various reasons for this, some of them were the fault of the Soviet rulers and some were not.

In 1967 the jubilee of the Revolution commemorated the achievement of a generation and a half and was intended to consolidate its basis in ideology. Yet the anniversary coincided with what is almost a national inquest on what has been happening to Russia since 1917. For several years this inquiry into the moral state of the nation has been carried out almost openly among the intelligentsia. Some probing books have been published, but the sharpest criticism is in the underground literature which now circulates extensively.

The writers are by tradition the guardians of Russia's conscience. In the nineteenth century there was little political life, the Church was either effectively muzzled or corrupt; so the prophets' function fell to the writers. In the twentieth century Stalin muzzled the writers almost as effectively as he muzzled the trade unions, but the writers are now asserting themselves again. Those who are too bold may still become martyrs, but there is a fairly good chance of survival, almost as good as in the nineteenth century. Some religious non-conformists have been tortured or killed. Literary non-conformists are more fortunate. They do, indeed, run grave risk of losing their livelihood. Some of them have been put in lunatic asylums, though they are perfectly sane. Others are in labour camps or in exile and bound to hard labour in an inclement region. For the secular intelligentsia the days of Stalin's Siberian *oubliettes* are over, but the punishment for expressing dangerous thoughts can still be severe. In labour camps with a "special régime" prisoners may still be forced to do heavy labour on a starvation diet of 1,300 calories a day; and they may be confined for very long periods to underground cells, where they sleep on cold concrete and may get no exercise or only a few minutes a day. It takes courage to speak out. So those who do have the courage are respected. Poetry recitations and recitals of new and perhaps "oppositionist" songs can be popular, like motor racing, as dangerous spectator sports.

The mood of the writers is better documented because writers write and what they write is evidence of what they think, but the scientific and technological intelligentsia are equally discontented. They are allowed to discuss dangerous thoughts and to listen to dangerous songs, so long as they remain within the ivory towers of a privileged existence in such places as the scientific township of Akademgorodok outside Novosibirsk. If, however, they put their names, for instance, to appeals with a political connotation, they are liable to be severely disciplined. But they are in a rather stronger position than writers and artists. The Kremlin knows it needs all the scientists it can get, but thinks that writers are expendable.

The immunity of scientists is, however, relative. Academician Sakharov is one of the most brilliant scientists in the world and is sometimes called the father of the Soviet H-bomb. Yet as I write these words in March 1969, news comes through that he has been deprived of his official positions, though remaining a member of the Soviet Academy of Sciences, for which he draws a salary. His offence was to write and circulate a radical memorandum on the dangers that the world stands in through the failure to apply science to "politics, the economy, arts, education and military affairs". And "we regard as scientific a method based on deep analysis of facts, theories and views, presupposing unprejudiced, unfearing open discussion and conclusion". It is said that after being circulated in draft and revised in the light of criticism, the document was presented, boldly or naïvely or both, to the Central Committee of the Communist Party. Scandalised, but not wishing to create a scandal, the Central Committee is said to have returned the document, saying, "You did not write this letter and we did not receive it." To which Sakharov replied, "Very well. You did not receive it, but I did write it. So now I am free to show it to anyone I like." Copies began to circulate, one of them was published in a Dutch paper, then picked up by the *New York Times* and eventually published in book form as *Progress, Coexistence and Intellectual Freedom* (Andre Deutsch 25s.)

Academician Sakharov does not spare his words. He speaks of "the rise of demagogic, hypocritical and monstrously cruel dictatorial police régimes. Foremost are the régimes of Stalin, Hitler, Mao Tse-tung . . . Stalinism exhibited a much more subtle kind of hypocrisy and demagogy, with reliance not on an openly cannibalistic programme like Hitler's but on a progressive, scientific and popular ideology. This served as a screen for deceiving the working class, for weakening the vigilance of the intellectuals and other rivals in the struggle for power, with the treacherous and sudden use of the machinery of torture, execution and informants, intimidating and making fools of people the majority of whom were neither cowards nor fools." "Not less than 10–15 million Soviet people perished from torture and execution in the prisons of the N.K.V.D. in the camps for exiled Kulaks . . . in the coal mines of Norilsk and Vorkuta from cold, starvation and the crushing labour."

He does not spare capitalist countries either, and concludes that "Only the competition with socialism and the pressure of the working class made possible the social progress of the twentieth century and, all the more, will ensure the now inevitable rapprochement of the two systems . . . The capitalist world could not help giving birth to the socialist, but now the socialist world should not seek to destroy by force the ground from which it grew. Under present conditions this would be tantamount to suicide of mankind." And writing just before "the Czech Events", Sakharov looked forward to a phased drawing together and mutual assimilation of east and west. It is the measure of the strength of his position that, even after this fierce criticism and open defiance of official views, the Kremlin did not venture to dismiss him for more than six months after his memorandum became widely known.

Sakharov does not stand alone. Constructive criticism of him, as well as approval and condemnation have come from inside the Soviet Union. One group, describing themselves as "numerous representatives of the technical intelligentsia", associate themselves with his criticism, but maintain that he does not go far enough. In particular "he places unreasonably too great hopes on scientific and technical means, on economic measures, on the goodwill of the leaders of our society, on the good sense of the people, and sees the basic causes of the world crisis as coming from outside our society. Here he is deeply mistaken, through sharing the basic prejudice of the age; he sees external causes and prefers external, material remedies, neglecting those that are internal, spiritual, political and organic.

"Economic growth, even the most rapid, cannot by itself miraculously ameliorate society and cannot eliminate social evils. If people aim to transform man, they are least likely of all to achieve this through his stomach. A well-fed wolf will never become a lamb." Presumably the group who write this are not disputing the desirability of some economic growth. They are denying its all-sufficiency. They write further, "The political upheavals of the twentieth century in our society have led to the removal of Christianity as a basic ideological force from the life of our society, and to the destruction of its moral values. The new materialistic ideology has not replaced (and could not replace) these lost values. A moral vacuum was thus created. In society this gave rise to morally split human personalities. On the one hand was a morality which was ostentatious, exterior, pseudo-collective, and on the other, a morality which was concealed, inner, primitively rapacious, egoistic. This created a society with a superficial, mechanical solidarity, but in fact, based on individuals alienated from society, fearful of their fellow men, feeling themselves lonely nonentities when confronted with the enormous government machine. In this kind of atomised society the sad phenomena which justifiably depress Sakharov are inevitable . . . Are we not placing too much blame on Stalin's demoniacal personality and his trusty 'cadres'? Society as a whole is directly responsible . . . An idol is inconceivable without idolators. Furthermore, should a new 'Stalin' appear, everything could repeat itself from the very start . . . Only the raising of our society's moral standards, of its conscious civic activity, and the awakening of a feeling of personal responsibility could effectively withstand such a bloody bacchanalia.

"For this purpose, new moral values, above all, have to be created. Our society must either work out or borrow, but in any case search for and find a new moral philosophical teaching.

"So far, evidently, it does not exist. But those who seek shall find!"

Such moods of discontent are widespread among the educated classes, but feelings differ greatly from one person to another, and discontent is hardly universal. There are certainly some tens of thousands and perhaps a hundred thousand political prisoners, taking the phrase to include all prisoners of conscience. Many more are exiles under conditions of varying hardship. These men and women have shown that they have the resolution to suffer for their beliefs, but it is impossible to say how much commitment and how much civil courage there is among the great majority who remain at liberty. However, it is at least becoming harder every year to restrain the free expression of opinion. In the last two or three years about half a million words of protest literature about the religious situation alone has reached the outside world. There must be many millions of words of "opposition" literature of one kind or another now circulating illegally inside the Soviet Union. Writers, scientists, various religions, and the minority nationalities are now at one in demanding a just enforcement of the existing laws; and sometimes they ask for changes in the law. But it should be emphasised that almost without exception their "opposition" is loyal opposition. So far as can be judged from outside, they are Soviet patriots who accept the socialist ordering of society without question.

The mood of the intelligentsia is more or less ascertainable, but it is an imperfect guide to the feelings of the workers or peasants, a subject on which there is little hard news. So far the peasants and workers are quiescent and seem to be apathetic, though from time to time news of strikes and go-slows filters through. But it would be dangerous to rely on the improvement in material conditions to keep them quiet indefinitely. In a country with such a passion for reading, what the writers think will inevitably percolate through to other classes. Moreover, in all ranks of society pride and cynicism are mixed in the same way: pride in their country's achievements, cynicism about the actions of all government authorities and disillusionment with the Marxist ideology that is supposed to underly the achievements. This attitude is not new. What is new is that these things are now openly discussed, even if the most damaging criticism is not yet published, and though there has been a tightening up since the fall of Khrushchev. So far the indications are that the working classes, being less closely watched than the intelligentsia, have rather fewer inhibitions about talking politics, when the subject interests them.

Soviet economic growth is slowing down. The easy profits of imitating the more advanced technology of other countries have now been taken. Further progress will depend on massive new spending on research, which will at first be a new burden on the economy. Moreover, the stability of the existing structure of society still requires enormous expenditure on matters such as housing and rural roads. The gap in technology between the Soviet Union and the United States is likely to grow and could grow to a point where it becomes intolerable to the generals. Yet more rapid economic advance is likely to be impossible without giving the scientific intelligentsia more freedom. It is on the cards that the Soviet Union may be drifting slowly into the sort of economic impasse that forced the Czechoslovakian Communist Party to initiate political reforms. The Soviet Union is now at last within striking distance of becoming an affluent society; but even now this achievement will not be easy. It is doubtful whether the Soviet Union is geared for advance into an economy of plenty. Her existing economic structure was designed to promote growth in an economy of scarcity, but now the expectations of her people are rising.

Yet, when all is said and done, most Russians are proud of their society, and there are some good reasons for this. From the old Russia they inherited a psychology of solidarity and co-operation that goes deep into the Orthodox past. And on the whole money and possessions take their just place in Soviet life, while the West continues to be obsessed with gain. There is plenty of greed and avarice in Russia, but the tone of society is set by those who like money and will work hard for it, yet do not hoard it. Insurance payments and hire purchase are marginal, and there are no mortgage payments. So money is spent as it is earned. Pensions are more or less adequate, except for the peasants, and no doubt the present gaps in the insurance system will be filled by degrees. Even those who have good reason to want changes in their own system may say, with a touch of superiority, "Yes. We understand that. In the West you can do nothing without money." This does not mean, in the cases I am thinking of, that they think westerners have no social services, but rather, that in our society you may have to fight for a margin of money before you are comfortable and can enjoy yourself without gnawing anxiety.

There is snobbery and ostentation in Russia but it is snobbery of position, not of birth or wealth, except in so far as wealth goes with position. What you are is considered more important than what you earn. One hears of "good families" but this is not part of the snobbery. A "good family" is one in which a good tradition is handed down. Finally, Soviet society has less of our modern cynicism than the West has. Good is good and evil is evil; and it takes no social courage to say so; but it does need political courage, if what one says is an indirect reflection on the system or those who work it. There are sick jokes in plenty about the sytem, but not generally about the ultimates of life. In spite of all, most Soviet citizens still believe in the future in a way that western man on the whole does not. "Socialism with a human face" would bring out the many attractions of Russian life that are often hidden below the surface, and by definition it would bring the end of tyranny and capricious rule. But is "socialism with a human face" what the Soviet Union is going to get sooner or later? It could be, but there are sinister forces on the other side.

Ideology may be stone dead, but many of those raised to power on ideological grounds have a strong belief that they have a sort of divine right to maintain their power, a mandate from history to impose order on a recalcitrant people, and to impose it by whatever means come handy. In the same spirit Tsarist officials treated criticism of any of their actions as seditious and almost blasphemous resistance against the divinely given autocracy. In a moment of irritation I once quoted to a Russian the sinister reactionary slogan which was the watchword of Nicholas I. "In the old days it was Autocracy, Narodnost (the quality of belonging to the Russian people) and Orthodoxy. So it was and so it will be again." I was surprised to hear myself say this, and even more surprised by the prompt "yes" which came in reply.

Since the mid-'thirties Russia's effective moving force has

been her national tradition. That is the Narodnost in this infamous trio. The Autocracy is threatened but as yet unbroken. Orthodoxy sounds like a long shot, but what is the alternative? What will take the place of the crumbling monolith of Marxism-Leninism-Stalinism? A plural society? Hardly. I doubt whether our current western ideas of pluralism in society are ultimately viable in any country, but, even apart from this, the whole tradition and psychology of Russia is against pluralism. They feel society's need for a coherent inspiration. For as far ahead as it is possible to see, Russia will have either an official ideology or a national religion, or perhaps an ideology allied with a religion. They are not the people to accept a spiritual vacuum. They will not settle down in a grey universe, where nothing has ultimate value. They read Kafka avidly, when they can get him, because their own experience is that of *The Trial* and *The Castle*, but they are not likely to take to the philosophy of Sartre: the category of "the absurd" as a fundamental of life is a thing they would never accept. Life must have a meaning.

But cannot something be rescued from Marxism? Stalin, indeed, is a discredited figure, even if the Party still dares not admit some of his worst crimes, such as the liquidation of the Kulaks, and even if a half-hearted attempt is made to rehabilitate him; but Lenin's memory is respected. One hears people say with pride, "Lenin has gone into history." Certain elements of Lenin's thinking have no doubt entered the blood-stream of the Russians, but Marxism-Leninism no longer commands serious attention among thinking people. Will a devotion to the early Marx with his concept of alienation take the place of a more rigid ideology? I doubt it. After an overdose of one kind of Marxism, it seems likely that some far more drastic swivelling round is in preparation and that, when the Russians eventually get their freedom, they will turn to something entirely different. Socialism indeed, in the sense of public ownership of the commanding heights of the economy, is fully accepted and will never be abandoned. It seems to be taken as self-evident that socialism is the right economic system, but the ideology that now goes with it and, still more, the extremes of its application,

are likely to be rejected root and branch. Liberal Marxism of
the modern variety may have a future elsewhere, but hardly in
Russia.

Russian nationalism is the one force that stands quite
unshaken, but this is a nationalism that is very conscious of
national tradition, and wherever you look into the Russian past
you find the Russian Orthodox Church. So, looking ahead
boldly, and perhaps rashly, to the time when the present
ideology will be not only dead but also buried, it is possible to
imagine the Russian Orthodox Church becoming once more
the effective unifying force of Russian society. But for this to
come true the Russian Church would have to outgrow its sometimes narrow nationalism which made it a force of division as
well as cohesion in the multi-national empire of the Tsars, and
could do so again. That the growth of an ideology based on the
Russian Orthodox Church is not an altogether academic
speculation is shown by the savage sentences on a group who
were tried in Leningrad in 1967–8 for conspiring to set up a
constitutional government inspired by the ideals of the Orthodox Church. Looking ahead, this possibility has attractions, but
an insidious danger is concealed. Russian nationalism has two
faces. There is a sound tradition of national life based on the
best in Russian Orthodox Christianity, but there is also "Great
Russian chauvinism". And this would be the natural mode of
thought for a home-grown Russian breed of Fascism, which is
also capable of claiming church support. Already in 1965 in
Leningrad a group of "Russkie Fashisty" were caught and
tried. But short of these extremes "Great Russian chauvinism"
crops up under any régime.

Under Soviet rule the minority nationalities have long been
required to delete from their history anything that reflects un-
favourably on their Great Russian big brother. In particular
those who resisted Tsarist conquest must be described as re-
actionaries. Sometimes the measures taken against the records of
minority national cultures have been extreme. In 1964 a large
part of the Ukrainian national archives were burnt. This was
arson and one of the employees of the library was convicted for

starting the fire. Many Ukrainians ask whether the arsonist was not acting on instructions from Moscow. A part of the archives which survived was in the monastery of Vydubetsky, near Kiev, which also was burnt in 1968. And other incidents which arouse suspicion could be given. To complete the picture, the Russians do also burn records of their own past. Every year large numbers of books and periodicals which do not fit official views are officially burnt. It is becoming very difficult to get copies of the works of many pre-Revolutionary philosophers and thinkers. The chauvinist element in the bureaucracy would, one suspects, find ready support both among the Komsomol (the official youth movement) and among the hoodlum element of the towns and villages. Youths brought up to the spectacle of government violence and lack of scruple may well grow up rootless and cynical. I do not wish to exaggerate but the growth of juvenile delinquency in the west of Europe raises far less anxiety than the corresponding phenomenon in the Soviet Union. And in the absence of reliable comparable figures, one must suppose that greater anxiety denotes greater cause for anxiety. It would be easy to document this from the Soviet press, but once again the best description comes from Solzhenitsyn who relates how what appears to be an officially organised group of young yahoos of both sexes harass a church's Easter procession:

> "The legal boundary to crime has not been crossed, the banditry is bloodless, the insult to the spirit is in the bandit leer of those grinning lips, the brazen talk, the courting, pawing, smoking, spitting two paces away from the Passion of Christ ... One old woman ... says to another: 'It's good this year — no hooliganism. Look how many policemen ...' So now we know. It was worse in other years. What then will become of these best of the millions we have bred and reared? ... What good can we expect of our future? Truly: some day they will turn and trample upon us all. And those who set them on us — they too will be trampled underfoot."

On any calculation, Russia's prison population is unduly

large. It must be remembered that in the accounts we have of concentration camps, the ordinary criminals far out-number the political prisoners. If, for instance, there are at present about a hundred thousand prisoners of conscience, it is a reasonable guess that the total labour camp population is of the order of a million, or about one in a hundred and fifty of the adult population. These figures are no more than an informed guess but halve them or divide them by three and they still remain formidable. Something is wrong with the social system of a country that puts even one in five hundred of its adult citizens behind barbed wire, or compels them to live in remote areas; and on the available evidence, a lower figure is unlikely. Either the social system breeds criminals in undue numbers, or very many people who are not criminals are exiled or put in forced labour camps.

It can easily be assumed that any radical change in the Soviet Union must be a change for the better; but it need not be so. People overthrew Tsarism, because they felt that anything would be better, but on a sober view it is doubtful whether what they got was not worse. When the inevitable changes in the Soviet Union do come, there are some grounds for hoping that they will be changes very much for the better. But it is possible to imagine a period of extreme Russian nationalism supported by a hoodlum mob and blessed by pliant hierarchs of the Russian Orthodox Church. Russian clerical Fascism would be ugly.

Such a system would, however, be unstable, for it would have against it the sometimes sullen and sometimes fierce opposition of that half of the population who are not Great Russians. And many Russians see the danger of their own patriotism getting out of hand. I give one instance. Though little of his work has been published in his own country, Solzhenitsyn is probably the most influential writer in the Soviet Union. With his love for the traditional Russian life, he stands in the Slavophil tradition; but he is at special pains to draw out the beauty of character shown by so many of the non-Russians in his writing. This sort of thing is not lost on Russian readers. Conforming religion is, indeed, a natural breeding ground for super-heated nationalism, but in the Soviet Union religion, whether Christian, Moslem, Jewish or Buddhist, is not conforming but persecuted. And in their persecution, Christians and others have discovered the universality of the right to freedom. They see that their own freedom depends on others also having freedom.

Is there any way of measuring the strength of conflicting beliefs? The inquiry is doubly hazardous in a country such as the Soviet Union where people have learnt so long and so thoroughly how to dissemble. Sometimes the words of Soviet citizens are little guide to their thoughts. And some of them have dissembled so long that they do not know what they think. This makes the burning honesty of many others the more remarkable. The one hard fact is that the Communist Party has about twelve million members; but it is only a minority of these who have any genuine ideological beliefs; how small this minority may be can only be known for certain when it is no longer advantageous to profess Marxist conviction, but I should be surprised if there are more than half a million convinced Marxists in the Soviet Union. On the other hand, there are tens of millions who, in spite of pressure, worship in church, when they can find a church that is open. The best estimate accessible to me is that the total Christian Community of all churches in the whole of the Soviet Union, including children of believers, is of the order of fifty million. Of course there are other religions too, but the great majority of religious people are Christian and among these much the largest grouping is the Russian Orthodox Church. If the numbers remain uncertain, it is at least clear that the convinced Christian minority is many times larger than the convinced Marxist minority, and that even regarding the matter purely from the perspective of this world, the Church is more than large enough to leaven the whole lump.

It must be hoped that when the great change comes in Russia it will be orderly and peaceful and that it will grow out of changes in the thinking of members of the Communist Party. The alternative of a period of chaos would be exciting, but it might leave things worse than before. There is, however, no reason why reforming leadership should not eventually come from the ranks of the Russian Communists, though it must be faced that this would almost certainly destroy the Party by destroying the ideology which is its one claim to legitimacy. Nowadays, if you hear some heterodox view attributed to someone and you say, "But isn't he a Party member?" you get an impatient answer, "Oh, that doesn't make any difference now." It is by no means impossible that the Party itself will throw up a leader who sees that the Party has become a liability.

What is almost certain is that when the change comes it will come suddenly. Russian government is a stiff, brittle structure with no give in it. It is cast-iron, not steel. So it never bends till it breaks. The Tsar was there one day and gone the next. Many people foresaw a revolution but no-one was expecting it. So it will be again, *mutatis mutandis*. Let us hope that the change will be as peaceful as the supersession of Novotny by Dubček in Czechoslovakia. But, however that may be, it will surprise everyone, including me. I do indeed predict that the change will come suddenly, but I am not expecting it now, and I know no means of predicting when it will come, except that with every year the hidden balance of probability tips increasingly to the side of change.

For the change to be decisive something of the order of a hundred thousand people would have to lose their jobs. Power could not be left anywhere in the hands of those who have grossly abused it, and many would have to go, but there are also a great many decent Party members and officials who have themselves committed no crimes and, if they have been accessories, have been so unwillingly and under great pressure. But those who rose under Stalin had to use Stalin's methods, while those who rose since his death could use milder methods. Unfortunately, many of the recent generation of leaders, including both Brezhnev and Kosygin, began their rise to power as young men during the Great Terror of 1937–8, when the way up was over the corpses of rivals and superiors. The generation of the 'thirties is still in power, and such men have much to fear, when the whole truth of Stalinism is revealed. Therefore they must repress free inquiry and refuse any public admission of the magnitude of Stalin's crimes. They may lose everything, if they lose their chairs; one may hope their eventual successors will as one of their first acts pass a very full amnesty for all that was done under Stalin; but one can see why, as a Russian has said, "they are holding grimly on to the seats of their chairs"; he suited his gesture to the words. However, in the nature of things, that generation are coming to the end of their time, and their successors will be less bound by a Stalinist past. So it seems reasonable to say that the great change will take place some time during the next fifteen years, at the end of which it will be more than thirty years since the death of Stalin. But the change could come quicker.

It will be asked what ideas are maturing in the meantime. No-one knows much about this. It is certain that far more thought is going on than the outside world has generally appreciated; the most interesting typescripts are not likely to circulate in circles that are accessible to foreigners and it is only occasionally that a corner of the curtain is lifted. But it can already be said that there is a good deal of interplay between the circles of ideas represented by science, Russian national tradition and the Orthodox Church. Is there, then, no dialogue between Christianity and Marxism of the kind that exists in the West? No. There is not. How can you have dialogue with a corpse? Or with the deceased's executors, when their idea of dialogue is to get you on the ground, sit astride on you, seize you by the throat and ask peremptory questions which must be answered "Yes" or "No"? Yet the forging of a new ideological or religious expression of Russia's social standards is a task that must be attempted. A mere rejection of Marxism, combined with the retention of a socialist economy and the acceptance of a national tradition based on eastern Orthodox Christianity will not be enough. I was at first sceptical of the value of dialogue between Christians and Marxists in eastern Europe—dialogue in the west is another matter. But I am slowly coming round to the view that there will be no "socialism with a human face" without prolonged dialogue, not with the official representatives of the Communist Parties but between some Christians and some of those who have been through Marxism. So far as I know, nothing of this kind has started in Russia. I do not see how it could be started till the ground has thawed a good deal more, but already the idea has been welcomed in principle by the Orthodox writers Leviten and Talantov and by the young Baptist Skripnikova.

The future will not be made exactly according to the ideas of intellectuals, but intellectuals have their part. It is they who give expression to the shape of events. Two men represent for me the old and the new generations of the Russian intelligentsia. Pasternak, whom I knew, represented the old generation who had been educated before the Revolution. Honourable, brave, sensitive and imaginative, he was unpractical, and was easily confused by the turgid eddies of an ambiguous situation, as was seen in his too innocent reaction to the events attending the award of the Nobel Prize to him. Solzhenitsyn, whom I do not know and am not likely to meet, is equally honourable, sensitive and imaginative, but even braver and far more practical. He has a toughness that was lacking in the older generation and he knows exactly what he is doing. The difference between the generations is the best ground for hope. Steeled in the terrible school of the concentration camps, Solzhenitsyn has had to find his own way from cynicism and unbelief. But the way of the Cross has led him to the foot of the Cross. I conclude with a prayer composed by him, which expresses the true ground for hope.

> How easy it is for me to live with You, Lord!
> How easy it is for me to believe in You! When
> my thoughts get stuck or my mind collapses,
> when the cleverest people don't see further
> than this evening and do not know what must
> be done tomorrow. You send down to me
> clear confidence that You exist and that You
> will see to it that not all the ways
> of goodness are blocked.

From the summit of earthly fame I look
round with wonder at that road through
hopelessness to this point, from which even
I have been able to shed abroad among men
the radiance of Your glory.

And You will grant me to express this
as much as is necessary. And in so far as
I am not able to do so, that means You
have allotted this to others.

LIBRARY OF DAVIDSON COLLEGE

Books on regular loan may be checked out for **two weeks.** Books must be presented at the Circulation Desk in order to be renewed.

A fine of **five cents** a day is charged after date due.

Special books are subject to special regulations at the discretion of library staff.